# LEGERING AND FEEDER FISHING

## Maurice Dutfield
## and
## Stuart Harford

Compiled and Edited by Dave King

**Beekay Publishers**

*Other angling titles by Beekay Publishers:*

*Coarse*

Carp Fever by Kevin Maddocks
The Art of Pole Fishing by Dickie Carr
Pike Fishing in the 80's by Neville Fickling
Basic Carp Fishing by Peter Mohan
Modern Specimen Hunting by Jim Gibbinson
Top Ten—tactics for the major species from ten leading anglers
Edited by Bruce Vaughan
Redmire Pool by Kevin Clifford & Len Arbery
Tactics for Big Pike by Bill Chillingworth
In Pursuit of Carp & Catfish by Kevin Maddocks
Cypry The Carp by Peter Mohan
The Beekay Guide to 450 Carp Waters
Jim Davidson Gets Hooked by Jim Davidson
In Pursuit of Predatory Fish by Neville Fickling
Tiger Bay by Rob Maylin
Understanding Barbel by Fred Crouch
Big-Water Carp by Jim Gibbinson
Mega-Pike by Eddie Turner

*Sea*

Boat Fishing at Sea by Phill Williams & Brian Douglas
Long Range Casting & Fishing Techniques by Paul Kerry
Cod Fishing by John Rawle
Uptide & Boatcasting by Bob Cox

*Game*

The Colour Guide to Fly Tying by Kevin Hyatt
Robson's Guide to Stillwater Trout Flies by Kenneth Robson
Dressed to Kill by Bob Carnill & Kenneth Robson

First published in 1990 by
BEEKAY PUBLISHERS
WITHY POOL, BEDFORD ROAD,
HENLOW CAMP, BEDS. SG16 6EA
© Beekay Publishers 1990
ISBN 0 947674 25 X

Typeset by BP Integraphics Ltd., Bath, Avon
Printed in Great Britain at The Bath Press, Avon

# Contents

# Introduction

By Dave King

I have always had a soft spot where legering methods have been concerned. As a boy, except when pike fishing with, in those days, the obligatory *Fishing Gazette* bung, most of my best fish were caught using leger tactics. At that time, the most sophisticated form of indicator was the rod tip or when night fishing, a half penny, or if we could afford it, a penny, balanced on the end of the rod with an Oxo tin underneath it. Bites would be signalled by the pull of the fish dislodging the coin which would then fall into the tin with a clatter. The technique was 'The' method of night fishing for carp on the Leicester canal. Once I left school and started out to work, I then joined the ranks of the 'posh' minority by investing in a 7/6d oil lamp to enable me to see my rod tip and respond to the bites more quickly.

My very first match win was also down to legering methods, although this was due to an accident of misfortune as opposed to any tactical decision on my part. Whilst night fishing the Friday before the match on that very same canal, someone stole my precious cane float rod that I had carelessly left on the bank behind me, so I was forced to use my 6 ft solid glass leger rod in the works match on Sunday. Casting my worm hook bait into a likely looking bay on the far bank of the Nene at Water Newton, I caught 2 eels and 8 Tommy Ruffe for a magnificent weight of 1 lb 4 oz, winning by a margin of 10 oz. This achievement was frowned upon by the Senior club members as, in 1962, legering was not considered a 'proper' way of fishing at that time.

Now, with the tremendous changes we have seen over the past 25 years or so in both bite indicators and rod development and the wide variety of techniques that have evolved from them, legering has an accepted and important role to play in modern match fishing methods.

In the late 1950's when the late Richard Walker said that a National Championships match would be won using leger tactics everyone laughed at him and told him he was talking nonsense. Now, in the last 30 years, more nationals have been won using legering and feeder fishing tactics than with any other single method. The big step forward in legering techniques was due to the development of the swing tip by Boston angler Jack Clayton. Although this type of bite indicator has now been superseded by modern quivertips, it did at the time transform legering and firmly establish it as a match winning method, and under the right conditions can still, on its day in the right hands, be the ultimate bream fishing weapon. The other big step forwards in this period was the introduction by Dick Walker of the Arlesey bomb. This gave anglers the ability to cast much greater distances and at the same time eliminate most of the tangling problems associated with trying to cast less streamlined leads at long range. The next important milestone was the development in the 1970's of the swimfeeder. Although this method had been around for a number of years previously, it was not widely developed to its full potential until that time. The last 10 years has seen an explosion in the development and marketing of specialist feeder rods and every season sees further refinements of the feeders and the equipment needed to fish them effectively.

The 2 authors of this book are brilliant all-round anglers, they have to be to fish for the Shakespeare Superteam. They are also great exponents in the art of legering and feeder fishing. Maurice Dutfield, in particular, has been at the forefront in developing the modern feeder techniques we accept as commonplace today. Both he and Stuart Harford have been travelling companions for many years, learning from each other and sharing the ups and downs of the match fishing circuit. Together they have a match record to compare equally with the best in the country and are committed anglers. Their achievements are too numerous to mention and like many top anglers of their calibre, when pressed to tell you of their match successes, can only remember the failures. This is not just down to modesty. Winning is a habit with them, so when they do fail, the failure, or to be more precise, the reasons for it, stick indelibly in their minds and the lessons learned filed away for future reference.

As with most aspects of match fishing with the running line, simplicity is the key to their success. This frees their minds to concentrate on what is happening beneath the surface and making the necessary adjustments to their tackle and feeding in response. They are totally confident in their ability, knowing under most conditions that they have got it right and if fish are not forthcoming then it is because they are not drawn on them. Although this book concerns legering methods and tactics, they are, when conditions dictate, used in conjunction with float fishing and pole fishing methods. They are certainly not used as last resort tactics as many anglers used to think in the old days. They are used when it is the correct way to present the bait in the prevailing conditions or when fishing at extreme range. As will be explained in this book they are applicable to a wide variety of venues from canals to broad rivers and from ponds to big lakes. They are particularly effective when fishing for the larger bottom feeding species, but in the right hands they can also be used for taking fish at various levels in the water.

When I took on the commission to write the match books in this Beekay series and The Shakespeare Superteam agreed to these no-holds-barred interviews, I knew I had the chance to produce something really 'special'. I was determined on behalf of myself and the other 90% of lesser mortals, not to blow it, and not to come away with a missed opportunity. As to the final result, only you, the reader can judge.

I feel that by keeping the interviews in the format of how they actually took place as opposed to re-hashing the material into normal book form, I will have kept the authoritative sincerity of the anglers concerned with regards to both content and fact. If your overall approach is transformed as much as mine has been after reading it, then I feel I will have succeeded.

Best wishes and tight lines!

# Profile: Maurice Dutfield

Like many top anglers, Maurice started fishing as a lad, going on trips with his father. Surprisingly, he did not take up match fishing seriously until he was 25, after, as he put it when his wife Gail was out of earshot, he had been married a number of years and the novelty had worn off. He concentrated his efforts on just a few local venues, the Severn, the Avon and in particular the Gloucester Canal. He began to succeed using a variety of methods and won numerous matches on these venues. He feels that any angler who takes up match fishing should follow this path, concentrating upon venues that suit their style and establishing themselves on them before travelling further afield. Due to his success, he attracted the attentions of the late Clive Smith, who at that time was the Captain of The Shakespeare Superteam and when the team was expanded in the early 80's to more than 12 anglers, Maurice was invited to join. Since then he has been one of the mainstays of the team, travelling to many venues much further afield with many notable team and individual performances. He says that once joining the team and with obvious personal pride that being invited gave him, he felt he had 'made it' and he has adopted a far more professional attitude to his angling; it has become an obsession as opposed to a hobby, and he is very grateful for the commitment and support of his family who he feels must have suffered, but who have still made many sacrifices in contributing to his success. He feels that due to the nature of the Superteam, being made up of anglers from many different areas, that this has contributed greatly to their success by sharing their wide variety of experience, skills and techniques.

For him personally, his greatest achievement came in the 1989 *Angling Times* Winter League Semi-finals, which the Superteam won and in which Maurice took the individual honours using pole and bloodworm tactics against the 'cream' of the southern pole anglers. The Shakespeare team were offered odds of 9–1 by the bookies, amplifying the top class nature of the opposition on this type of water. Maurice is justifiably proud of the way that they, as underdogs on this venue, came out on top as both a team and him personally for taking the top individual weight.

# Profile: Stuart Harford

Stuart has been fishing ever since he can remember and has always loved the sport. He used to go and watch his father fishing in the local open matches and he himself started competing at open level from the age of 15. He won 3 junior Championships in Worcester but modestly says that looking back, the methods used were very basic and he feels fortunate that he had the draws to encourage him. He had his first senior open match win on the River Severn at Stourport at the age of 16 and had a number of successes prior to getting married.

As with many successful young anglers in the past, married life initially had a very restraining effect upon his fishing and he was forced to drop out of the match scene for a few years until he and his wife Sue had got settled and put a home together. After he had settled down he took the sport back up again. Encouraged by Maurice and by travelling together, sharing the bait and transport costs and also the winnings, he started again to make an impact in his local area, winning the Wye Championships for the first time in 1976. Several seasons later he joined the Birmingham Starlets match group and enjoyed continual success as both a team member and as an individual. He was a member of the Captain Morgan Cup match winning team in Ireland in 1983, and as an individual won the Gloucester Canal Championships in 1982 and the Wye Championships for the second time in 1983. He continued to fish for the Starlets for 8 years, but increasingly found that due to their particular team policy at that time, which tended to concentrate on canal and still-water venues, he was too restrained as to the variety of fishing he could do and when he was invited to join the Shakespeare Superteam after being nominated by Maurice, and Dave Harrell who was also a former Starlets team member, he was only too pleased to accept. The more liberal policy of the Superteam in the fact that they encourage their members to take part and succeed in open events as individuals, to help maintain form and confidence, has brought him 'back to life' as he puts it, and he continues to go from strength to strength. Like Maurice he takes great pride from the fact that he has been asked to fish for the Superteam, which as they both acknowledge is the angling equivalent of being asked to play football for Liverpool. He is also fortunate in having the support of his family in his commitments, and looks forward to many more successful years at the top.

The 1989/1990 Shakespeare Superteam.

Maurice feeder fishing on the Warwickshire Avon at Twyford Farm.

Maurice striking into a fish on his local lake.

Stuart Harford displays his match-winning catch of 28 lbs 14 oz of carp caught from the Birmingham National Exhibition Centre lake, using long range floating maggot tactics at a distance of approximately 80 yards. To cast his leger to this distance he used a 1 oz bomb in conjunction with a 13 ft float rod.

The editor Dave King netting a good tench caught on caster and groundbait feeder tactics using his favourite swingtip indicator.

# The Shakespeare Superteam

The name 'The Shakespeare Superteam' needs very little introduction to anyone who knows and partakes in the sport of match fishing. Since their formation they have always been the team to beat if success is to be assured and have always been at the forefront of angling achievement. Their consistency has always been based upon having the cream of current angling talent amid their ranks, and this being encouraged and directed to its full potential by the team Manager and Captain, Ken Giles. The strength of the team lies in the fact that it consists of a strong and resolute core of individual anglers. This may sound like a contradiction of terms, but Ken is certain that this quality of individualism is what makes them so consistent as a team. Their general all-round ability, combined with their individual approach to the various methods required to be utilised under a variety of conditions, is what makes up their awesome collective strength. Over the years names have changed and new talent has been brought forward and encouraged, ensuring a continuity in results virtually unequalled in match fishing history. Team championships and competitions are a development of the last decade and will be at the forefront of angling in the future, whatever that future may bring. The days of the secretive individual were numbered once the format of the old 'All England Championships' was altered from an individual and team weight, to a team points system. Professionalism has now taken over and no team typifies this approach more than the Superteam. Under the banner of Gleveum AC they have risen through each of the divisions annually to achieve their rightful place in Division One of the NFA Championships and it is only a matter of time before the title of Division One Champions is assured.

I will now let Ken take over and tell the story of the team's conception and what he considers to be the key to its success.

**Ken**: In 1973, Clive Smith and myself approached various tackle companies with a view to financial sponsorship. At that time this had never been done before and was a totally new concept with regards to angling. A few top anglers had, in the past, associated themselves with tackle companies and put their names to various products, but no-one had approached anyone with regards to actual cash sponsorship to represent the company on the match circuit.

Most of them laughed us off and said that this sort of thing can never happen, but one company, Shakespeare, did not dismiss us out of hand. We had a couple of meetings with them and they did show some interest. They saw that Clive and myself were getting fairly consistent results and they saw that there could be something in it for the benefit of the promotion of the company and, of course, for Clive and myself.

In the end they decided to sponsor us and in return we were given a free hand in the development and design of specific products for the match angler and these became very successful. The Match International range of rods and reels became very popular and out-sold other companies' Match fishing products during this period.

Up to this time, major angling matches and events were tailored to individual weight performance and what few team events there were also concentrated on total weight to decide the outcome. Apart from the National Championships, these were mainly aimed at 4-man teams, and would run a 4-man team prize as a supplement to the major prize which was aimed at individual performance. Again these would be decided on a total weight basis, but each man would draw as an individual. At this time there were no sectional draws for the team event.

To try to make our mark under the system as it stood, we were allowed to recruit 2 more members into the sponsorship arrangement with a view to entering the team events. These 2 were Max Winters and Tony Davis.

This lasted for several years and we were quite successful as both a team and as individuals.

Eventually, due to the increased interest and publicity generated by the success of ourselves and other teams such as the Leicester Likely Lads and the Starlets etc, team events became more popular and in some top events these were expanded for teams of 6. To be able to take part in these and also to give ourselves a pool from which to field a 4-man team regardless of illness, holidays etc, we recruited another 2 anglers: Dave Williams and Steve Webb.

Currently, only 3 of the original 6 are still fishing. As most people know, Clive sadly died, and Max Winters and Dave Williams have both since given up fishing totally. This was a great loss to angling, but unfortunately these things inevitably happen.

By this time, team fishing, as we know it now, was rapidly being developed. The introduction of the points system in the National Championships was adopted for the winter and summer league events and many of these now catered for teams of up to 12 anglers. Due to the success we had achieved, and the effect this had on tackle development and sales, the Shakespeare Company allowed us to expand our squad to its present level of 14 anglers, from which a strong team of 12 can be selected at any one time, with regards to current form and strengths on each particular venue. It also helps with things such as holidays and work commitments, occasional health or family problems etc. If we only had 12 members and due to a car breaking down or sudden illness we were a man short on the day, as a team we would be dead. So by having a squad of 14 we can always be certain in a 12-man event of fielding a strong team.

There have been a number of changes over the years. For various reasons anglers have lost form or, due to working or matrimonial pressures, have been unable to maintain their commitment to the sport, and it is my job as Captain and Manager to maintain the continuity and strength within the squad. All the squad members are very experienced, successful individual anglers within their own right, but when we fish as a team they are committed team anglers.

The selection of the team on the day is my decision alone. None of the team are consulted or need to be concerned with team selection. There are times when I have the unpleasant job of telling a team member he is dropped, due to lack of form etc, but my decision is always unquestionably accepted and with good spirit. This policy is, I feel, the best for the morale of the team in the long term. I do not agree with systems where teams are decided by selection of a committee or by consultation. If that same enthusiasm was shown on the river bank as is shown around a bar when discussing and selecting team members, these teams would win everything going. Instead I think they are negative and divisive.

Such is our relationship and commitment that I rarely have to make the decision to drop an angler for a particular match. If, due to loss of form or any other reason, any of the lads feels he should be dropped for a particular match, he will normally approach me with this view in mind, as opposed to me approaching him. Should this happen, I know I can still count upon him turning up on the day, if asked, to run the bank and give us 110% effort in collating and passing on the necessary information to the team.

One of our greatest strengths is that our team consists of a majority of mature anglers who are settled in their life-styles and have the full support of their families and employers. This is essential if you are to give the degree of commitment necessary to succeed. Many anglers can do this over a period of 2 or 3 years, but to maintain this over a period of 10 or 12 years, despite the pitfalls that they will inevitably come up against, means that these men are exceptional. They are something special and I am proud to have anglers of this calibre in the team. They are the key to our continual success.

# Rods and Reels

Q   *What types of rods do you use for legering and feeder fishing, on stillwaters and canals at close and long range?*

**Maurice:**   For all of my close range legering on stillwaters and canals, I use a Sigma Wand. This is a 9 ft rod made from glass fibre and has a very nice soft through-action, essential for use with the fine 1 lb breaking strain hook lengths that we need to use on occasions. The rod has 3 different length tips, the longest being the softest and most sensitive, and the one we use most. (See Fig. 1) It is a lovely rod to use and is suitable for all light leger and small feeder work for roach and smaller bream, and is my first choice for fishing venues such as the Gloucester Canal, where both of these species are encountered. To my mind, carbon fibre is totally unsuitable for this type of fishing. As I have already mentioned, the softness of the fibre glass is essential to prevent cracking off on the strike when using fine hook lengths, and also helps when playing fish on very small hooks. The shock absorption qualities are essential to minimise the risk of the hook pulling out, especially at the critical stage of netting a good fish. I find carbon far too stiff for these particular situations. It is important to have complete confidence in your equipment, whatever your preferences and I have total confidence in this particular rod for that particular type of fishing. The only criticism I have of it, is that due to the very fine eyes on the quiver tips, during freezing conditions these tend to ice up very quickly and this often results in the tips snapping off at the ends. I keep meaning to get a spare tip to re-ring it with larger eyes for use in the winter, but I still have not got around to doing it yet, particularly as these last 2 winters have been so mild and I have not experienced the problem as much.

**Stuart:**   I also use the Sigma Wand for light legering and feeder fishing, but for longer distances, where we need to cast larger leads and feeders, I use the Team Carbon Multi Tip rod. This has a range of 4 tips, and can be used for light to medium feeder work on both stillwaters and

Fig. 1. Fine Wand tips.

rivers. With the 2 longer tips it makes the ideal long range bream fishing rod for stillwater fishing and with the shortest tip it is powerful enough to handle those hard fighting Severn barbel. This rod is 11½ ft long, a length that is essential for long range casting on stillwaters, and for holding the line well up when fishing flowing water.

The only other rod I use for stillwater legering on such venues as Arrow Valley lakes, where I am long distance fishing for carp, is surprisingly a 13 ft float rod! I find this essential for casting the 60 to 70 yd necessary and the indication is no problem with a species such as carp. The extra length helps to cushion the viciousness of the bite and also gives me greater control over the fish. The larger rings allow for the use of a shock leader, which is also essential when punching a feeder out at that sort of range.

**Q**   *What types of rods do you use for feeder fishing and legering on flowing waters?*

**Maurice:**   For light feeder fishing and legering with weights up to 1 oz, the Team Multi Tip described by Stuart is ideal. When used with the shorter tip it can cope with a reasonable amount of flow, the type normally found on the Warwickshire Avon and the middle Severn during the summer months. I have had a lot of success with this rod, particularly with the smaller blockend feeders that I have been increasingly using just lately.

For medium feeder work I use a rod that I have adapted from a 12 ft President float rod. I have cut 5 inches from the bottom of the butt and re-ringed it and, for me, it is the perfect medium feeder rod for weights up to 2 oz. It is not much use for straight legering, except when meat fishing for barbel on the River Severn when it is carrying extra water. Then it really comes into its own with the heavier tackle. Under these conditions I would be using up to 2 oz leads on a 5 or 6 lb line, but primarily it is a feeder rod. For straight legering on flowing water with maggot and caster baits, I would use the Multi Tip, as I can vary the sensitivity of the tips to suit the conditions.

Although I have constructed the medium feeder rod to suit myself there are commercially made rods on the market which are just as good. But this particular rod suits me and the way I fish and, again, I have had a lot of success with it and I am totally confident in its performance. This, as I have previously mentioned, is the essential consideration no matter which rods you choose for particular purposes.

It is essential with modern legering and feeder fishing techniques to have a range of rods to cover the different weights of feeders and for use on still and flowing waters at various distances. The range of rods now available from the different manufacturers is endless, and preferences vary from one angler to another and from one area to another.

We can only tell you what we use, bearing in mind the wide variety of venues which we fish. It is then up to the individual to identify the qualities he is looking for in a particular type of rod and then to practice with it until he knows its qualities and limitations intimately and is confident in getting the best from that rod for the job it is specifically designed to do.

**Stuart:**    There is another rod we use if we are feeder fishing in a big powerful river like the Wye, where you need the big ski leads attached to the feeders to hold out in the flow. This is the Team Carbon Feeder rod, which is designed to cast up to 4 oz of lead. This is a really powerful rod, very stiff and you are unable to use less than 3 lb hook lengths with it or you will continually crack off. But it has its place for these sorts of conditions. Also, it is very useful on the Severn or the Trent when there is a lot of extra water coming through, and you need to hold out in these conditions. Contrary to popular belief, fish do still move about and feed well out in the river under these conditions and can often be attracted to big baits such as luncheon meat and lobworms.

Another thing I tend to do as well, such as when we fish the Sundridge league at Winnals, where you are casting a fair distance, fishing the far bank for chub and using 1 lb and 1½ lb hook lengths and small hooks, is to use a spliced tip float rod such as the new Shakespeare Kevlar as a Medium feeder rod. Being 13 ft, it allows you to fish the far side, keeping much more line out of the water than you could with the lift rod. This makes for far more positive indication and the extra length helps to cushion against the take of a good chub on such a fine hook length.

As Maurice has said, it is important to understand and recognise the qualities you need for the various types of waters and methods, and select a rod to do that particular job. Unlike float rods, where one type of rod can be used for most float fishing situations, legering and feeder fishing does demand a suitable range of rods to cope with different situations. Years ago, before modern legering and feeder fishing techniques were developed, the average match angler could get away with having just a couple of rods, one for stillwater fishing and one for fishing rivers. These days, at least 4 different types of rod are needed, along with the ability to recognise when and how to use them. This is essential if you are to succeed on the match circuit. Confidence and faith in the ability of your equipment to cope with all conditions is essential.

Even now, we still see anglers struggling to make inadequate tackle perform properly. Either they cannot comfortably reach the range at which they need to fish, or they are unable to see the bites properly or are continually being broken by big fish. It is difficult to achieve a balance between a rod that is capable of casting a 2 oz feeder, and being able to play a large chub or barbel on a fine hook length and small hook.

**Maurice:** Even now we still sometimes get it wrong. There are occasions when even we find we are being cracked off by chub and barbel before we even have time to lift the rod off the rest. In these situations you have to step up the strength of your tackle, knowing full well that you will encourage fewer bites. But what is the point of getting bites if you cannot land the fish? New methods and equipment are being developed all of the time and to be successful you have to keep abreast of them. Having said that, the simplest methods are always the best when you can use them and hopefully these will be fully explained later on in this book.

**Q** *What types of reels do you use for legering and feeder fishing and what features and rate of retrieve do you prefer?*

**Maurice:** The reel I use is the 040 Sigma Graphite. It is a very good, well constructed, smooth reel. In fact I like it so much that I use it for everything, legering and float fishing. The big advantage of doing this is that I can carry a number of bodies around and know that all my various spools with different types of lines will fit them, and in the unlikely event of a reel jamming up or spring breaking on the bail arm, I can unclip the spool, replace the reel with another and be instantly back in action. The only thing I would say is that I wouldn't like to subject them to a lot of hammering by casting and retrieving the big heavy 4 oz feeders. For this sort of work I step up to the 050 size, using 5 lb or 6 lb line, or use an older non-graphite Sigma 040 which I carry around specifically for this type of heavier work on the upper Severn or on the River Wye and sometimes on the Trent if it is pulling hard.

**Stuart:** I basically use the same except for when I am fishing the Wand. On this I prefer to use the smaller 035 size, I feel this balances the rod better. Obviously when fishing for bigger species such as chub or carp I use the same as Maurice. I cannot see the point of using a closed faced reel or a reel with an automatic bail arm for legering and feeder fishing. The problem with any automatic system is that, should it fail, especially when feeder fishing, you are going to crack off on the cast, which is expensive in both the loss of equipment and in loss of time under a match situation. By opening the bail arm manually you know it's open, and providing you pull on your line to check that it's free before each cast, you should never crack off. Another point that I think is important and would like to cover at this stage concerns the anti-reverse lever. We always fish with this in the 'off' position, allowing the reel to instantly back-wind if we connect with a big fish. We never use this or the clutch system. These reels are very smooth and it is very easy to feel the fish through the gearing. Normally on the strike the fish is running with the bait anyway and if you had this lever in the 'on' position you would be continually cracking off at your hook length.

**Maurice**:   With regards to the gear ratios, the majority of reels on the market these days have a retrieve rate of about 5-1. If used sensibly, this presents no problem and is very useful if a fish runs towards you and you need to rapidly take up slack line. Under normal retrieving and fish playing situations, providing you take your time and are careful, line twist situations can be minimised. Obviously if you start winding your tackle in too quickly you are going to risk line twist and tangles. This will happen under this situation whichever gear ratio you were using. The important thing is to be able to identify when this situation is likely to occur and with experience you can counter it. The main thing is to keep your terminal tackle as simple as possible, avoiding ironmongery and complicated set-ups. This will also help to minimise the risks of tangling.

# Line and Hooks

**Q** *We all have preferences in the brands of lines we use, but what qualities do you find essential for legering? What breaking strains do you use for legering and feeder fishing?*

**Maurice:** The most important consideration is line stretch. It is essential to use a line which will stretch well. Most mono-filament lines come into that category. The line I use is Shakespeare Omni. It is a perfect line for most aspects of angling. It stretches well and has a good knot strength. The stretch is important for 2 reasons. One, it gives you a degree of shock absorption when casting a heavy feeder, and 2, it helps to cushion the strike and protect your hook length when you connect with a big fish. You always use a lighter hook length and if you are going to break it will always be on this.

By having a high degree of stretch in your main line as well as your hook length, it does help to take some of the shock, reducing the risk of cracking off. Although Omni is classed as a floating line, for most river fishing this does not present a problem, as you fish with the rod up in the air anyway.

When fishing stillwaters and canals in windy conditions it can be a handicap and under these situations I would either treat the line with washing-up liquid to help make it sink, or switch to using a fast sinking line such as Maxima, but where possible I do prefer to use Omni.

**Stuart:** An older line will always sink anyway, so what I tend to do is keep a line that has been used for float fishing and then use it for legering, bearing in mind that I change my float fishing lines after about 6 outings, so they will not have had a lot of use anyway, but they will be prone to sinking which is why I change them. It is essential when stick float fishing to have new lines that float well. These will of course be the finer lines used for straight lead and small feeder work on the Sigma Wand. When using medium and heavy feeders I will of course be using heavier lines from 3 lb to 6 lb breaking strain. In most cases these do not present a problem when winding down to a heavy feeder, but I also carry spools loaded with Maxima for those very windy conditions on still waters and canals when I want the line to sink very quickly.

**Maurice:**  We always try to match the main line with the size of feeder we are using. When fishing with the straight lead up to ½ oz or one of the mini stillwater and canal feeders, a 2 lb or 2½ lb breaking strain line is more than adequate. This would be used in conjunction with 12 oz to 1½ lb breaking strain hook lengths. When feeder fishing on the Warwickshire Avon and the lower Severn in the summer months when the rivers are at normal summer level, a 3 lb main line is quite adequate, again using 12 oz to 1½ lb bottoms for the smaller fish or with 2 lb bottoms for chub and barbel when they are biting freely.

If we are straight lead fishing for barbel and chub using big baits such as luncheon meat or lobworm, a 4 lb line with a 3 lb hook length would be used under normal conditions, but in really snaggy areas we may step up to as much as a 6 lb line with a 4 or 5 lb hook length. When using the big heavy 3 to 4 oz feeders in strong flows, a 5 or 6 lb line is essential for casting and retrieving these, but the hook lengths will only be 1½ to 2 lb when using small baits for average size fish. If we are expecting a larger stamp of chub or barbel this would be stepped up to 3 lb. As with the main line, these hook lengths will always be of a high stretch mono-filament such as Omni or Bayer Perlon, to prevent the fish from cracking off on the take, as can often happen when using a heavy feeder. What happens is, the fish swims off with the bait at high speed and when it pulls against the weight of the feeder it can often break the hook length, unless it is cushioned by the give in the line. In these situations it is essential to trim the feeder so that it only just holds in the flow. Then, when the pull of the fish hits the feeder it will move, causing the rod tip to fall back and give slack line to the taking fish. All the angler needs to do is to tighten gently up to the fish, which will have hooked itself. If you strike under these conditions you will invariably crack off at the hook length.

**Stuart:**  As well as matching the main line strength to the size of the lead or feeder, it is also important to match the hook length strength to the hook size.

A size 22 or 20 fine wire hook on a 3 lb hook length is totally wrong. The hook will be grossly overloaded. At the other extreme, you cannot expect to drive home a size 8 hook when meat fishing, on a 1½ lb hook length. If you need to use a heavier hook length when larger fish are around, you must step up your hook size to suit. We will be covering hook types later on in the chapter.

**Q**  *When, if at all, do you advocate the use of shock leaders when feeder* *fishing or legering?*

**Maurice:** When feeder fishing at distances in excess of 40 yards I will always use a shock leader. On stillwaters I will use a 5 or 6 lb leader, attached to a 3 lb main line. When river fishing a 7 or 8 lb leader would be used with a 4 or 5 lb main line. It is important to have at least 5 or 6 turns of the leader on the reel spool when the feeder is in the normal casting position, which is usually about 3 ft below the rod tip. Under these circumstances the use of very fine tips is out of the question. The more powerful rods that we have discussed already would normally be used under these conditions.

**Stuart:** When casting at these sort of distances, even with the relatively small capacity feeders that we use on stillwaters, I normally use a spliced tip float rod. The extra length and action allows you to reach the distance comfortably and the larger rings allow the knot where the leader joins the main line to pass through easily with the minimum of resistance. Normally, under these circumstances, the target species are large fish such as carp and bream on stillwaters, or chub and barbel on rivers, so indication is no problem under these situations. Although on some waters, the size of the feeder may be relatively small, the weight attached to it will be stepped up to enable us to cast to the required distance comfortably, as will be explained in the chapter on feeders.

**Q** *What hook patterns do you use for the various species and baits and how do you vary these to suit changing conditions?*

**Maurice:** The hook is the most important part of your tackle. It is the first thing after the bait that the fish will see or sense. Its weight rather than its size is the important consideration and to get the bait to act as naturally as possible. It is important to use the lightest, strongest hook you can with regards to the species you are after and the breaking strain of the line you need to use to get bites. Out of the dozens of different types and patterns available on the market, it is important to keep the number you use down to the bare minimum to cover the various situations you are going to come up against. By doing this you will get to know their various qualities and limitations and know what you can and cannot get away with using under very difficult conditions. When the fish are feeding confidently, it obviously pays to use the biggest, strongest hook possible to take advantage of this situation, but when bites are few and far between, you may be forced to use a smaller, finer pattern than normal to induce bites, but by knowing your hook's limitations you can often get away with this, providing the water is relatively snag free and you take your time when playing the fish. As we have said before, it is pointless hooking a fish if you stand no chance of getting it out. Under these circumstances you will have to use a size and pattern that may mean fewer bites, but over the course of the match put more fish into the net. Only experience can teach you which is the best balance of probabilities.

The types I use for the various species are as follows. When chub fishing on venues such as the Warwickshire Avon, the middle Severn or the Trent, I use the Mustad 90340 barbless in the new odd size pattern. The normal sizes I used, depending on how the fish are feeding, would be sizes 23, 21 or 19, when fishing with maggots. These would be fished in conjunction with 1 lb to 2 lb hook lengths, depending upon hook size and bite response. When fishing for roach or skimmers I would use the Kamasan B520 whisker barb in sizes 24, 22, 20 and 18. These would, due to their fineness, be used with 12 oz to 1½ lb hook lengths. I would not normally use these for chub fishing or with lines heavier than 1½ lb as they are very fine and straighten out too easily under these circumstances.

For large bream, big chub, barbel and carp I use the forged Kamasan pattern, the B920. These are very strong hooks and I would use these in sizes 22 down to 16, in conjunction with 1½ lb to 3 lb breaking strain hook lengths. If I find I need to go down below 1½ lb hook lengths to get bites, I would use a Mustad 90340. Again it is most important to get the balance right.

The only other pattern I use for legering if I am using luncheon meat or lobworm, is the old pattern Mustad 39302 in size 8 or 6. I believe the number has now changed to 486. I still have a large number of boxes of the old pattern in stock. This is a fine wire hook, but it is also very strong. The fine wire ensures good penetration which is essential when using a large pattern. It is important if you get a good batch of any hooks, to buy as many from that batch as you can afford and keep them in stock. The quality can vary from batch to batch. I remember buying some hooks that I had great faith in previously, only to find that they kept snapping off at the bend. For some reason the temper on this particular batch was faulty and the hooks were too brittle. I went around a number of dealers before I found one with a good batch in stock and bought a large number to put into my personal store. By the time these were used up, the problem had been sorted out and the new stocks were back up to the standard I had come to expect. It is important to check hooks for strength and temper before leaving the shop. The worst time to find out you have a batch of faulty hooks is during a match. I always use the first of a new batch during practice sessions to prevent this problem from happening.

**Stuart**:   Basically I use the same patterns as Maurice, but when I am fishing for bream on stillwaters I prefer to use the Drennan Caster Blue hooks in sizes 16 and 18. In these sizes it is a nice big hook with a long shank which allows for the use of 2 or 3 small red worms or worm, maggot and caster cocktails. The hook is very light which is important when bream fishing as you often have to sit on your hands and let the bite develop. Despite the frustration of this, once the fish has taken the bait you often find the hook is well inside the fish's mouth when using these hooks, so it is obvious that the fish does not detect its presence. The fine wire does ensure good penetration, so providing you play the fish carefully, there is little chance of pulling out.

When fishing in Ireland, where you often end up 'speed fishing' for big bream, under these conditions you need to use a forged hook to bully the fish out. In these circumstances I would use the Kamasan B920, often in sizes 14 and 12. But in this country, where the target weight is often only 20 or 30 lb you have the time to play the fish carefully and I have great confidence in using the Caster Blue.

It is important to keep it as simple as possible and not get confused by using too many different patterns of hooks. The ones we have mentioned do cover all the aspects of match fishing that we come up against and providing you recognise the situations where you can use a light hook and when it's essential to use a strong forged pattern, you will not go far wrong by using the types we have covered. Obviously, if you use and prefer different patterns to those we use, and have confidence in them, then it is pointless to change. But if you have been experiencing problems with hooks in the past, then by all means give these a try, and if they work as well for you as they do for us, then great, we are only too pleased to have been able to help you through the maze.

**Maurice**:   Modern hooks are a lot more uniform now than they used to be. Not so long ago, before the modern types came onto the market, you would buy a box of 50 hooks and due to various imperfections you would perhaps only be able to use about 20 or so of them and end up throwing the rest away. The size of the spades would vary considerably as would the length of the point, and you would end up having to go through the whole box sorting them out. Now, happily, this situation no longer arises to the same extent and, providing you check a few from each box at the point of sale, you can be fairly certain that if those are alright the rest will also be usable.

As we have already mentioned, hook penetration is the crucial consideration. It is vitally important to check that you have a razor sharp point. This may not always be visibly apparent, but it can be felt when putting the bait on the hook. If the hook goes through the bait cleanly and easily without bursting it, you can be pretty sure that the hook is alright. If at any time during the course of the session you feel that the hook point has curled or been blunted with use, you must change it immediately. Nothing kills a swim quicker than a hooked fish coming off. Sometimes this is unavoidable due to the bait coming back over the point, masking it, but if the point has been blunted for any reason you will notice this when you come to put a fresh bait onto the hook. If you have any doubts at all you must always change it.

**Stuart::**   These days with the use of barbless and micro-barb hooks, hook penetration is far superior to what it used to be. You know that when a chub picks up the bait and hits the feeder as it swims off, 9 out of 10 times all you have to do is pick up the rod and release the reel spool with your finger and the fish will have hooked itself. You do not have to strike to set the hook like you had to in the old days. This results in far less crack offs than we used to experience, which can only be good for both the fish and the angler. In the rare event of being broken, you can at least be comforted by the thought that the fish will be able to get rid of the hook quickly and easily, and I cannot recall a single occasion in the last few seasons where I have caught a fish with someone else's hook still in its mouth.

# Baits

Q  *What baits do you use for legering and feeder fishing under normal match situations and how does their introduction vary for different types of waters and species? Do you prefer to breed your own hook bait?*

**Maurice:**  For most of our fishing we use maggot and caster baits. These are the back-bone of the match anglers bait requirements. Having said that, by virtue of the fact that we live on the banks of the River Severn at Worcester and consider this river to be our 'home venue' we probably use luncheon meat far more than anglers in other parts of the country. This still is the premier bait for big barbel if there is colour in the water, and on many sections of the river these are the target species, especially during the summer months, if a winning weight is to be put together. We do, of course, also use maggots and caster in conjunction with hemp-seed as barbel baits as well. However, when they are 'on the meat' you will always use it in preference to maggot and caster baits because it does allow you to use heavier tackle, which is always an advantage with this very hard fighting species. Barbel are now also beginning to show in increasing quantities on the River Trent, so I can see a chance in the very near future when our methods will also be applied successfully on this river as well.

   As I have already mentioned, hempseed is the key to barbel fishing regardless of which other baits are used in conjunction with it. This summer on the Severn we were using an average 6 to 8 pints of hempseed per match and this would be spread between 2 lines of the river, 4 or 5 pints would be introduced on the near line by hand or catapult, and 2 or 3 pints would be introduced by means of a feeder out in the main flow. In conjunction with this you would also introduce a few pints of casters, spread between both lines, and alternate with caster or luncheon meat on the hook.

**Stuart:**  It's surprising how quickly hempseed and casters are washed out of a block-end feeder on flowing water. Many people think that because you need to use ground bait in an open-ended feeder to introduce these baits on stillwaters, that the same applies to flowing water. This is just not true. Casters and hemp are washed out of a block-end feeder very quickly, in a matter of seconds rather than minutes, and it does not take long to put down a good carpet on a strong flowing river like the Severn.

On many occasions you can see when the barbel are moving into the swim. As they feed on this carpet of hempseed, they send up clouds of small bubbles similar to tench. It is always a thrill to see this happening, as you then know that the fish are there and feeding and it is only a matter of time before they find your hook bait. On some occasions when the river is running low and clear you can actually see the individual fish moving over the feed and you can inch the bait down under their noses. When this happens, it pays to leave your line slack to prevent them from cracking you off as they take the bait, especially when using casters on a lighter line.

One point about using luncheon meat. Many anglers use cubes of bait on the hook, but we prefer to use flakes. The bait is cut into long thin strips and we break off the pieces as we need them. We normally cut the bait up at home and take it to the venue in plastic containers. This prevents the risk of empty tins being left at the water side which, as well as being unsightly, can also be very dangerous, not only to your fellow anglers but also to livestock coming to the water's edge to drink.

We also use hempseed in conjunction with caster when roach and bream fishing, but obviously not in such vast quantities. It is a superb attractor and holding bait for most bottom feeding species and we always take some with us, especially during the summer months.

**Maurice**:  With reference to whether we breed our own hook baits; if we know we are going to catch bream we always breed our own gozzers. Skimmers especially love gozzers, but they must be very fresh. Certainly no more than 2 days old. The advantage of breeding your own is that you can take them off the feed at various sizes. Sometimes you can catch well on a double small gozzer, about the size of a pinkie, at other times you can do well using a single large one. The small gozzers used to work very well on the Gloucester Canal in conjunction with squatts and casters in the feed. In the summer matches on this particular venue, it was a waste of time going on the match without gozzers. We would use a double sized pinkie gozzer with squatts and a few casters in our ground bait, alternating with a larger gozzer or a caster on the hook when bites on the double small gozzer slowed down. In these situations we would use a very small open-ended feeder, casting it right across and under the far bank.

Many people consider the breeding of gozzers to be a very smelly

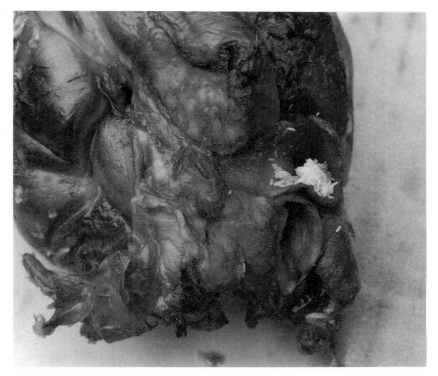

Fig. 2. Fly 'blow' in artery of a sheep's heart.

anti-social process, but if it is done properly, no problems with wives or neighbours should arise!

Normally 2 types of meat are used to produce gozzers: sheep or pig's hearts or chicken portions. Some anglers prefer to use a whole pigeon, but these are not always readily available. It is essential that only the gozzer fly blows on the meat. Fortunately a characteristic peculiar to the gozzer fly is that it will only lay its eggs in dark or very dull places. The meat should be put into a biscuit tin or similar container with a couple of inches of fresh bran covering the bottom. Slits are cut in the meat if chicken is being used, and the meat is laid on top of the bran. If a whole pigeon is being used, the beak is kept open by wedging it with a piece of matchstick, as the fly normally lays its eggs in the pigeon's throat. It is not necessary to pluck it. If hearts are used the fly normally blows in the opening of the artery (see Fig. 2). The tin should be placed in a dark corner of a shed or garage and the window or door left slightly open. Another method is to place the tin under a dustbin lid which is held up by a small block of wood or a stone. The lid should be left resting on the top of the tin so that only a small gap large enough for the fly to enter is left. During warm, dry weather, you should get a blow on the first or second day. In cold, wet weather, it may take 2 or 3 days to get a blow. Weather conditions not only affect the time taken to get a blow, but also the hatching and growth rate of the maggots. In warm weather, the whole process from first putting down the meat to the maggots reaching full size only takes 6 to 7 days, but during cold conditions it could take from 10 to 14 days. As the bait needs to be used within one or 2 days of coming off the meat, timing can become a problem. If you intend to ensure you have a regular supply of gozzers for both week-end and mid-week evening matches and practice sessions, by organising yourself and regularly putting down meat every Saturday and Wednesday during the summer and autumn months, you should always have fresh fully developed gozzers on match days, regardless of the vagaries of the climate. Also, by having regular bait breeding taking place, the flies will tend to hang around the area, thereby speeding up the time taken to get a blow.

Never throw unused bait away. By scattering a few of the gozzer casters in the corner of the shed or garage, fresh breeding stock will hatch at regular intervals. Some anglers even go to the extent of building mini fly houses, feeding the flies on sugar to make the blowing process more efficient and certain. Once the meat has been blown, it should be wrapped in newspaper. Use about 5 or 6 sheets keeping them altogether as opposed to wrapping it in separate sheets. This makes periodical inspection much easier. The parcel is laid on the top of the bran inside the tin and the lid tightly closed. Plenty of air holes will be needed in the lid but these must be kept small, or rouge flies will lay their eggs through the holes. I prefer to cover the tin with a pair of lady's tights instead of a lid. This allows more air to circulate.

After about 3 days the parcel should be opened and the contents inspected. Provided the weather is warm, the maggots should be about half grown and feeding well. This is the time to put in any colouring if you want to colour feed the bait, and extra meat if you think the feeding maggots will need it. If colouring powder is to be used this can be sprinked dry onto the meat, as the juices caused by the feeding maggots will activate the dye. If annotto is used the roll must be cut up and melted in hot water to form a yellow paste and then applied to the meat with a brush. The parcel is then re-wrapped, placed back into the tin and covered with fresh bran. When the maggots have reached full size they will finish feeding, leave the remains of the meat, and work their way through the paper and into the bran. When this happens the contents of the tin should be tipped onto a wire mesh riddle, allowing the maggots

Fig. 3. Special bait box with cut out lid used with floating maggots.

to fall out of the meat. They can then be riddled off from the old bran and cleaned with maize meal. After a couple of hours they can be riddled again and put into a small bait box containing damp bran and placed in a cool place or in a refrigerator. This will prevent excess dehydration of the gozzers. If they are left in dry maize meal they will shrink and toughen. All the waste from this process can be put into a plastic bag and the end tied to seal it. This will prevent any bad odours emitting from your dustbin.

This procedure sounds very complicated, but the only difficult thing about it is convincing yourself that you can do it successfully. Once you have tried it and found how easy it is, there will be no stopping you in the future. You will always have a regular supply of good quality hook baits and will find that it is not just bream which like gozzers. All species will accept them readily and you will increase your catch rate, especially when conditions are hard. Another advantage is that gozzers also tend to be lighter than commercial maggots and are ideal for fishing on the drop. They will fall more slowly through the water and counter the weight of your hook.

**Stuart:**   One bait that I find essential for bream fishing is red worms. Often, one or 2 worms, either on their own or used in conjunction with a cocktail of maggots or casters, can be a deadly bait for big bream. I keep a well watered compost heap in my garden, inside a wooden frame. Into this I put all my grass cuttings, kitchen waste and some well rotted farm manure and this makes it an ideal breeding ground for red worms. By keeping it well watered, but not soaked, during the summer months, I always have a readily available supply of red worms of all different sizes.

One point that I feel is important to mention: you must never use grass cuttings from lawns that have just been treated with weedkiller or fertilizer, or weed and feed treatments. You must wait until after at least 4 or 5 cuttings before you can use them again or you will kill off all of your worms.

On some days the bream will want a single large worm, on others a bunch of tiny red worms is the bait to use. It is important when bream fishing to keep ringing the changes between these and different coloured maggots, gozzers and casters in all sorts of combinations. When using bunches of worm or a single worm on the hook, it is important to hook them through the head or the saddle and thread them over the spade of the hook and onto the line, holding them clear of the hook with a caster or maggot (see Fig. 4). This ensures that they cannot come back over the hook point, masking it on the strike. Many a good fish and many a match has been lost in the past, due to this happening.

Sometimes a bunch of squatts will do the trick. One dodge that works on occasions, is to use a larger hook in conjunction with a paste made up from your ground bait. This can often work well on heavily fished waters where the bream know they can safely consume large amounts of ground bait without getting hooked. Whatever bait you use, it is essential that it is as fresh and as clean as it is possible to be. Good quality bait is essential and we put a lot of effort into its cleaning and preparation. As soon as I get my bait home from the shop I riddle it off, removing all the old bran or sawdust and any dead maggots. If the bait is already dyed I will put in plenty of fresh maize meal and put them in a big bowl in the fridge. Small or narrow containers are no use for storing bait. These will make the maggots sweat and smell. If I need to dye the bait with chrysodine I will put the maggots into a container clean and neat with no maize meal at this stage. I will then sprinkle the chrysodine powder onto the bait and leave it for a few hours. I then go back to the fridge later on and add a few handfuls of maize

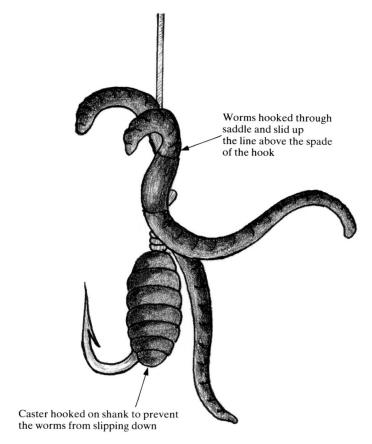

Worms hooked through
saddle and slid up
the line above the spade
of the hook

Caster hooked on shank to prevent
the worms from slipping down

Fig. 4. Correctly hooking redworms to prevent them from masking the hook point.

meal and leave them in this overnight. The next morning, before the
match I will riddle them off again. By this time all of the excess dye
will have been soaked up by the maize meal. I then transfer them into
my bait bucket and add some Tumeric powder, followed an hour or
so later by another couple of handfuls of maize meal. This ensures that
the maggots are in perfect condition. During the summer months, particularly after a long drive to a match, I will repeat the process at the bank
side, again using Tumeric and maize meal.

I also clean and prepare any shop bought casters the day before
a match. Many anglers buy a bag of casters and just put them in the

fridge overnight without opening the bag until they get onto the bank. I never do this. I always empty the casters out onto a sheet of paper and sort through them to remove any dead skins and those shrivelled-looking black-fly casters that may be present. I then transfer them to a clean bait box after removing a handful to turn overnight into floaters, for use on the hook. The bait box should be filled to within a quarter of an inch of the top, then a plastic bag is put over the top and trapped in position by the lid. This makes it airtight, so that the casters will remain sinkers. I then put it in the fridge overnight. This prevents the problem of 'bag burn' which is a common occurrence when casters are left overnight in a plastic bag. The handful of hook baits are put into a small container with the lid left off and also put into the fridge, where they will darken gradually overnight. The advantage of using a floating caster on the hook is that it counters the weight of the hook and is buoyant enough to be sucked up off the bottom naturally by the feeding fish. Fish seldom pick a bait up with their lips, they just suck on a bait and if due to the weight of the hook, or the stiffness of the line, the bait does not rise like the loose feed, they will just ignore it and pass on to the other offerings. This is another reason why gozzers score well. They tend to be that bit lighter than commercial maggots and rise off the bottom easily. Also, due to their softness, the fish will then tend to hang on to them that little bit longer.

**Maurice:** Going back to the subject of worms, one of the best stand-by baits for when the river is carrying extra water or under normal conditions on occasions, is the lobworm. Chub especially like lobworms and if you feel certain that you have chub in the swim, but they are not being very responsive to maggots or casters, it can often pay you to go out on a straight leger with a big lobworm on a size 6 hook. Chub tend to be sight feeders and they very rarely ignore a large tasty morsel such as this. You can use a heavy lead and wind down to it, presenting the worm still on the bottom, or you can use a lighter weight and bounce the worm through the swim. Anglers are now winning matches with chub on the River Trent by setting their stall out to fish the lobworm right from the start of a match, especially since the use of wasp grub has been banned in many of the matches. Some of the chub shoals on this river are massive, with many of the fish running from 1 lb plus. It does not take many of these to start building up a good weight. Twelve or 15 fish can give you 20 lb plus, which is only averaging 3 fish an hour. With such a big wide river to go at, this can often be a comfortable target to achieve if you draw on fish.

**Stuart:** I have to agree, I use the lobworm a lot on the River Wye when I am unable to catch on the float or feeder. I always take a good supply with me when I fish this river. I recently came second on the Wye Championships using lobworms, although on that day the target species was eels. The river was carrying a lot of extra water and conventional feeder or float tactics using small baits was out of the question. The best lobworms are those taken from the surface of lawns at night. These are the biggest, softest lobworms, far superior to any that you get by digging. During dry conditions in the summer, I always water my lawns well in the early evening to be certain that the worms will come up to the surface when it gets dark. I have tried storing lobworms in special beds in the garden, but they are virtually impossible to keep in good condition, so I have no alternative but to go out with the torch an hour or so after it gets dark. With care they can be kept for a couple of days in the summer months, so I always prefer to get them then, rather than being up until after midnight the night before a match, especially during the summer when they seem to refuse to come up until the early hours of the morning.

In the summer I keep the worms in a bucket of damp moss. This is kept in a cool part of the garage. This will keep them alive for up to a week if it is not too hot. It is important to check them daily and remove any dead worms. Because the worms do not actually feed on the moss, it scours them out and toughens them up making them nice and firm. This ensures that they stay on the hook properly when casting at long range. In the winter I use strips of newspaper which have been well soaked and then squeezed gently out. You can keep them safely up to 2 weeks like this which is very helpful, particularly if you have a prolonged period of frosts. The worms do not come up to the surface when it's frosty and you can often get caught out due to this when you need worms for a match. Obviously your own lawn will not be productive enough to keep you supplied all the year round, so it is important to find places such as parks and grass verges, or neighbours lawns with their permission, to use when necessary.

**Q** *What importance do you attach to the use of additives and colourings to your maggots and casters?*

When carp fishing, I sometimes use a few additives in my ground bait, but to be quite honest I don't think it makes any difference. Some people have a lot of faith in them, but I feel that providing your bait is clean and properly presented, if the fish are feeding they will take it. I have tried them on my bait, but always as an after thought on hard days to see if they encourage the fish to feed. Despite using various types of flavourings, they have continued to be hard days. If by using them, they give you confidence, then all well and good, but there is nothing magical about them and in no way are they a substitute for ability.

**Maurice:**   I think what happens is that people try them and by coincidence they have a good day and put this down to the use of the additives. They probably would have caught just as much on that particular day anyway, if they had not used an additive at all.

I am confident enough in my ability to know that if I draw on fish and they are feeding I will catch them. At several pounds a bottle, I just cannot jutify the expense when measured against the results and I think they catch far more anglers than fish.

To me it's just another blind alley for the inexperienced angler to go down when he should be concentrating his efforts on the real issue of improving his techniques.

Colourings do make a difference, particularly on hard fished waters. On the Trent and the Avon the bronze maggot has been far superior to white maggots for many years now, having said that, in certain places the red maggot has been the 'in' bait. I have caught a lot of fish this last season on 'Disco' coloured maggots. These are varying shades of slightly fluorescent orange and bronze and for some reason these always feel a little bit softer than other types of commercial maggots. We tend to feed mainly with bronze maggots, but put a few reds and Discos in with them and use them for hook baits. The thing to do is to keep experimenting and never slavishly stick to one particular colour.

**Stuart:**   Maurice keeps raving on about these Discos and I keep trying them, but I think I have yet to get a fish on them. For most of my fishing I use bronze maggots; if I think I am going to catch bream I also take red maggots.

One tactic that we sometimes use when bream fishing, but more often when carp fishing on venues such as Arrow Valley Lakes, is to use floating maggots. Half an inch of water is put into the bottom of a bait box and a handful of maggots put in and left overnight prior to the match. The maggots will take in the water and this makes them float. We make special lids for these containers as, obviously, when the maggots get wet they can climb out of the bait box, but you cannot keep messing about taking a conventional lid on and off every time you change your hook bait. What we do is to cut a hole in the centre of the plastic lid of the bait box just big enough to get our hand in. In an average sized bait box this leaves about 1½ inches all around the outside of the lid (see Fig. 3). Any maggots that crawl up the side of the box will fall off the lid back into the box before they can reach the opening. Obviously an un-cut lid is used when transporting the bait and the special lid is used in its place whilst actually fishing. Floating maggots are also useful when chub fishing on canal and river venues where this species is present. One or 2 maggots will be suspended in the water above the leger at whatever length you make your tail. This can be a deadly method in the summer when these fish are sight feeding up and down the far shelf at all levels in the water, but are not feeding on the bottom.

**Q** *What types of ground bait do you use and how does its make-up vary for different types of waters and species and also for the different methods of introduction, ie hand throwing, catapulting, or for use in swimfeeders? How much of a part does the use of specialist ingredients and additives play in the make-up of your ground bait? What degree of importance do you give to the colour of your ground bait?*

**Maurice:** Most of our ground bait medium still consists of basic white or brown crumb, blended together or used on its own, depending upon the nature of the mix we require. If we are fishing a deep, powerful river such as the Wye you need to make your ground bait like concrete. To achieve this we use two-thirds white to one-third of brown, with a bit of crushed hemp to help bind it. It must go straight to the bottom very quickly to keep it in the confines of the swim and once it is on the bottom it must hold, breaking up very slowly. To achieve this we must make sure it has soaked in the maximum amount of water, so we always mix it over wet and then 'bring it back' to the right consistency by adding a little dry ground bait if necessary, although normally, if we wet it well before we tackle up, by the time we are ready to use it, it will have absorbed all of the water and be about right. I always prefer to add my ground bait to the water to ensure that it is thoroughly and evenly wetted. When fishing a stillwater, say for bream, we want a mix that will hold together whilst being thrown, but will break up on impact with the surface creating a falling cloud of ground bait and squatts or casters. On deep water, we would want the ball to start breaking up at mid-depth; to achieve this we use mostly brown crumb with little or no white. The amount of white used will vary with the depth of water. The deeper we want the ball to go before it breaks up, the more white we will use. If we want the ball to break up on impact we will use very little or no white at all. When feeder fishing with ground bait on stillwaters, we seldom use any white at all. In these circumstances we would use plain brown ground bait with very little water added. This drier mix then explodes out of the feeder as it absorbs the water after casting.

You will need to experiment and try different ratios of mix before you get it right. The amount of water absorbed will also alter how the mix performs. For very long distance ground baiting, the more water you add the heavier the mix will be, which is of course an advantage helping you to reach where you intend to fish. The way the ball breaks up is then controlled by the proportion of brown to white used.

In recent seasons I have also started using Van den Eynde Super Cup and Secret, mixed with traditional fine brown crumb. This gives me a very well textured mix and the bind of the mix can be altered by varying the amount of brown crumb used. Again only practice and experience can help you to get it right.

**Stuart**:  I tend to mix my ground bait the opposite way. Adding the water to the ground bait. I don't think it really matters which way you do it, just as long as you make sure that it is mixed evenly and, for hand throwing, that the crumb has absorbed the maximum amount of water. Like Maurice, I tend to over-wet it and then 'bring it back' to the dampness required. For stillwater work where it is important to have a soft fluffy mix, I always riddle it well after mixing to remove any lumps and to make sure it is nice and fluffy.

With regards to using continental mixes, I am still in the experimental stage with it and I am still not certain as to whether or not there is any advantage in it. When I won the Birmingham Parks matches I also used a bit of it, but I am also pretty certain that if I had used just plain brown crumb I still would have won.

A few years ago Timmy Aplin from Nottingham won everything going on the leger, and his ground bait had so many additives in it you could almost get high by sniffing it. Everyone thought 'Tim has got this superb mix', and it really seemed that he had got it right. He was winning or getting high places all over the country, which seemed to point to the fact that he really had something. But the important thing was that he was also getting the draws. Last season, despite continuing to use his 'magic mix' he has done nothing. The reality of the draw bag has caught up with him and this goes to prove that if you are not on fish you cannot catch them. Obviously, he was catching well when he was on fish, so he must have had something right and of course he was confident in what he was using, which is all that matters. But like the bait additives we talked about earlier, there are no magic ingredients. The secret, if there is one, is to keep it basic. Get to know your mixes and how they work with regards to throwing, catapulting and breaking up etc, and be confident in them.

**Maurice**:  One thing that is important is that you must always wet your hands and glaze your balls of ground bait before throwing or shooting them out. Make up your 6 or 10 balls that you are going to put in, then wet your hands and glaze them. This is always better than making one up, glazing it, throwing it in and then repeating the process with each individual ball.

There is nothing worse than the balls breaking up in mid-air, scattering and falling short, though it happens to us all from time to time. When using a Whopper Dropper you must use a nice even pull, lobbing the ball out gently. Try to force it and it will break up and scatter (see Fig. 6).

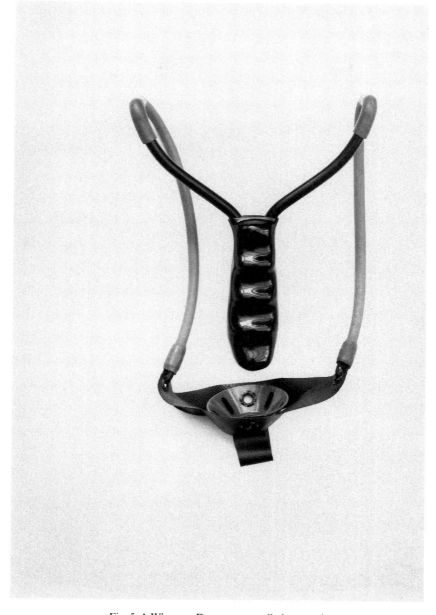

Fig. 5. A Whopper Dropper groundbait catapult.

Fig. 6. Stuart Harford using a Whopper Dropper to good effect.

As we have already mentioned, it is also important to use a much drier mix when introducing ground bait with a swimfeeder. If you put in a sticky wet mix this will not come out of the feeder until you start to retrieve it. This is the worst thing that can happen, as it will start coming out halfway between yourself and the baited area, again scattering the feed and the fish all over the water. Again, when casting a feeder, a nice smooth lob will give you just as much range and ensures that the feeder hits the water gently with the ground bait inside. Cast fiercely and you risk the feed being forced out of the feeder in mid flight, again scattering the feed all over the place.

One benefit of using a feeder is that you can put in far more squatts or casters per volume of ground bait than you can when hand throwing or catapulting, and it is very important to take advantage of this. Not only does it mean you are introducing a greater number of particles into the swim, but it will also make the feeder lighter and cause less disturbance as it hits the surface, an important consideration, especially on canal venues.

With regards to colouring, some venues, mainly clear waters, do seem to respond well to red ground bait, or to be more precise, it is fashionable to use this on these particular waters. Yellow ground bait is also used by some anglers in well coloured waters. I do use red ground bait on occasions, particularly when bream fishing on clear waters. I use the colouring powder available from tackle shops and add it to my conventional ground bait mix. Whether it improves my catch rate I don't know, but I have confidence in it and as we have said before, that is all that really matters.

Don't forget — discarded line kills birds and other wild animals

# Terminal Tackle and Rigs

**Q**  *Many patterns of swimfeeders and feeder systems, some incorporating interchangeable weights and trim leads are now available on the market. Which types do you prefer for the various aspects of feeder fishing? What modifications do you make, if any, to commercial feeders to improve casting accuracy and to minimise the risk of tangling?*

**Maurice:**  The development of the swimfeeder has come on in leaps and bounds over the last few years. Many firms are now getting it nearly right and most of us now use commercial feeders. In the early days the range was very limited. The open-ended feeders came in one or 2 sizes and the block-end feeders were the same as the open-ended type, with the addition of a cap on either end. These were normally flat caps that put up a great deal of resistance in the water and you would end up by playing both a fish and your feeder against the current at the same time. The lead size was uniform, with one strip of very thin lead attached to one side of the feeder, and to hold out in any sort of flow you had to buy sheet lead and cut off your additional strips, adding these to the feeder until it held where you wanted it to. The current range of additional leads was not available at the time.

Eventually the requirements of the match angler filtered down to the manufacturers and slowly but surely things began to improve. Even so, all sorts of weird and wonderful designs came on to the market to be accepted or rejected by the anglers and, like the situation we came up against with the float explosion of the 1970's, more were designed to catch anglers than fish.

Feeders for maggot fishing on stillwater venues eventually got smaller, but the weighting systems were still prone to tangling and did not allow the feeders to be cast with consistent accuracy. The linkage systems for attaching the feeders also left a lot to be desired and we normally discarded or modified these before they could be used properly without the use of excess ironmongery. The systems we use today are

so simple, it seems incredible that it has taken so long for the manufacturers to get it right.

Whilst all of this was happening, the more serious-minded of us
could see the potential of the feeder as a method, particularly with the
decline in response to the traditional ground baiting tactics employed
at that time. We started to either make our own feeders or adapt the
better of the commercial patterns to suit our requirements. Gradually,
a pattern emerged as to how best to overcome these problems and make
feeders to suit the different venues and species. The main problems we
encountered were with the size of feeders. Whilst many were fine for
the bigger rivers such as the Severn and Trent, they were too large and
cumbersome for canal fishing and stillwaters. Eventually, by cutting down
the Drennan feeder links and altering the weighting and linkage system
we arrived at suitable mini block-end feeders. The mini open-end feeders
we made up ourselves by cutting up the commercial open-ended feeders,
and to give you some idea of the size, we were making 4 canal feeders
from each standard commercial feeder! I ended up as official feeder-maker
for the Shakespeare Superteam. I had made up a series of moulds for
casting my own range of leads and these were attached to the feeders
by means of clips on the larger ones or by sticking them on with super-glue
for the smaller ones. Eventually these got passed on to Peter Drennan
and other manufacturers and now good commercial patterns based upon
our requirements are available on the market and the time taken up making these 'specials' has been reduced considerably.

My basic river block-end rig is shown in Fig. 7. The nylon or metal
link from the commercial feeders is removed and the feeder is reversed,
so that the detachable cap is at the bottom. An 8 inch length of nylon
mono-filament is passed through the centre of the feeder and a small
bead is tied to both ends. These are the tiny beads used to make decorations
on material. This is then threaded onto the main line and allowed to
run freely up and down the line and is stopped above the hook length
with a small No 8 or 6 shot. I use this system for chub or bream fishing
on both still and flowing waters.

For roach fishing with a small block-end, I use a slightly different
method. I still use line threaded through the feeder, with a bead tied
to the bottom and a small swivel tied to the top end, but the link only
extends about 1½ inches from the top of the feeder. The removable cap
in this instance is at the top of the feeder. A rubber insulation sleeve
is slid over the line above the feeder and covers all but the top eye of
the swivel (see Fig. 10). This helps to keep the cap secure and prevent
tangles. This is then tied to the 8 inch link of a standard paternoster
rig (see Fig. 8). Over the years I have found this rig to be ideal for roach
fishing, again on still and flowing water. The feeders normally stay the
same size with regards to capacity, but the weight is varied to suit different

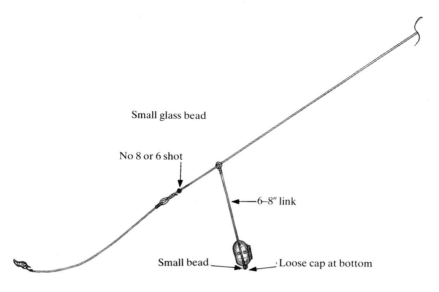

Small glass bead

No 8 or 6 shot

6–8″ link

Small bead

Loose cap at bottom

Fig. 7. Maurice's basic feeder rig.

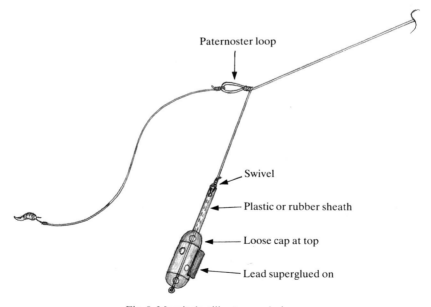

Paternoster loop

Swivel

Plastic or rubber sheath

Loose cap at top

Lead superglued on

Fig. 8. Maurice's stillwater roach rig.

casting ranges or rates of flow in rivers. Special small capacity feeders are used in the winter time or, on other occasions, when I only want a very small amount of feed to be introduced.

The small open-ended feeders that I use when bream fishing on canals and stillwaters with ground bait and squatts, are attached with an 8 inch link to the flap in the top of the lead strip by means of a small loop. A small bead is tied to the top and these are fished like the first block-end feeder, running free on the line with a stop shot above the hook length.

**Stuart:**    Tackle firms such as Drennan and Thamesly now make an excellent range of feeders. They are tailor-made for the match angler and I tend to use them straight off the shelf without any major modifications. I buy the full range of interchangeable leads and trim weights that are now available and these enable me to set up the feeders to suit a variety of conditions and I can get on with them quite well (see Fig. 13).

My terminal rigs also vary to what Maurice uses. When feeder fishing, I prefer to use the double loop system (see Fig. 11). This has several advantages over the running leger. Firstly, it acts as a bolt rig when a fish runs with the bait and as the end of the loop hits the feeder it hooks the fish for you. Secondly, it prevents the feeder running down the line and away from you when you need to fill it. This often happens with a running leger. You put the rod on the rest whilst you change the bait on the hook and the feeder slides down the line towards the rod tip whilst you are doing this. You then have to mess about lifting the rod to slide it back down the line towards you before you can fill it. With the double loop system this does not happen. The feeder automatically comes to a stop when it reaches the end of the loop.

Another advantage is that when you cast the rig, the weight of the feeder cocks the small loop outwards, holding the hook length away from the main line and reducing the risk of it tangling (see Fig. 12).

One system that is very popular with northern anglers, although we do not use it, is to use Power Gum links either fixed under the flap of the lead, or through the centre of the feeder. I cannot see the advantage of this, but it is a very popular method on the Trent, so I feel that it is worth mentioning (see Fig. 15). A small bead or a small piece of biro tube is slid onto a length of Power Gum. This is then twisted together by turning the ends in opposite directions and it is then threaded through the feeder and knotted. Alternatively, a shorter length is used, knotted and then clipped under the flap. It is claimed that this acts as a shock absorber for both casting and when a running fish hits the feeder. I have yet to be convinced by this, but these lads use it to good effect and have great confidence in it, which is all that really matters. The thing is to practice with the various rigs we have discussed and see which method suits you best.

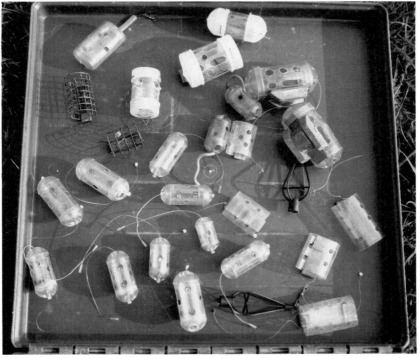

Fig. 9. A selection of Maurice's feeders.

Fig. 10. A couple of Maurice's cut down mini feeders. The one on the right is adapted for roach fishing.

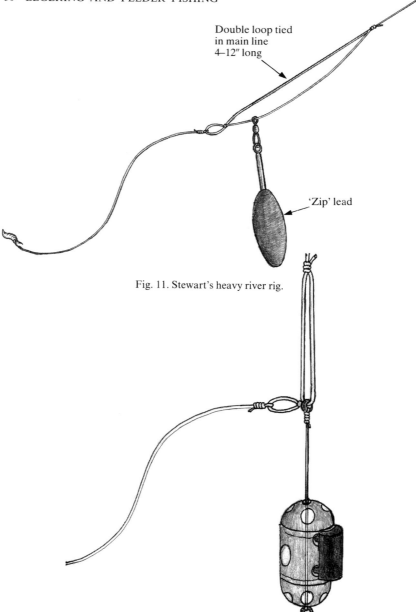

Double loop tied
in main line
4–12″ long

'Zip' lead

Fig. 11. Stewart's heavy river rig.

Fig. 12. Lower loop cocked outwards by weight of feeder preventing tangles on the cast.

Fig. 13. Interchangable weights and trim leads.

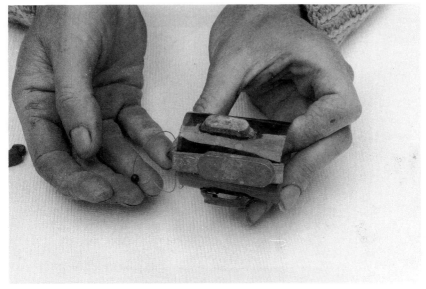

Fig. 14. Making up a large groundbait feeder for fishing in heavy flows.

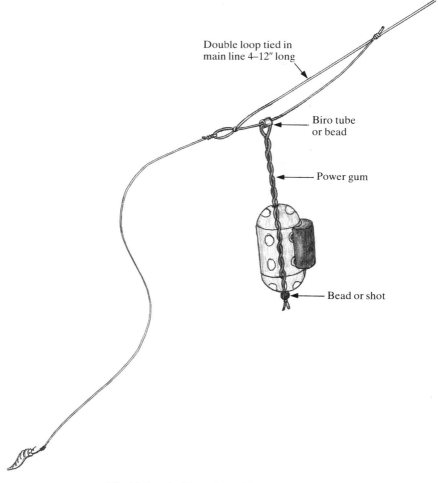

Double loop tied in
main line 4–12″ long

Biro tube
or bead

Power gum

Bead or shot

Fig. 15. Popular Trent rig used by northern anglers.

**Q** *What rigs do you prefer for straight legering and how do they vary to suit different conditions? Which of the new non-toxic leger weights do you find the best to use?*

**Maurice:** For bream and roach fishing, I always use the fixed paternoster rig. This has been proven over the years to be the simplest and most effective rig for this type of fishing. A small loop is tied 8 to 12 inches

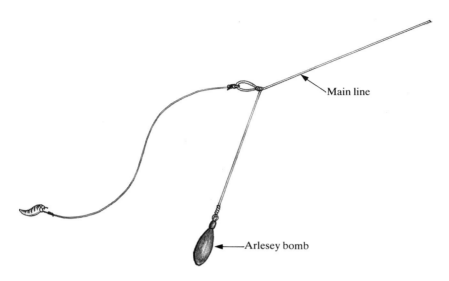

Fig. 16. Maurice's straight paternoster rig.

up the main line and to this you attach your hook length (see Fig. 16). The leger weight is then tied to the end of the main line. The hook length is varied to suit the conditions. In the summer months when the fish may be feeding at all levels in the water, this can be as long as 6 ft. In the winter months, when the bites are shy and the fish are taking the bait on the bottom, it can be reduced to 2 to 3 ft in length to give a more positive indication. The 8 to 12 inch link is normally used on still or slow-moving waters and this can be reduced to 4 to 6 inch when used in faster flowing water. When bream fishing, the breaking strain of the hook length seldom exceeds 1½ lb in snag-free waters and for roach I seldom use a hook length heavier than 1 lb.

For larger species such as chub, carp and barbel I prefer to use a running link leger, due to the fierce nature of the bites. This is the same as my running link feeder rig, but a bomb replaces the feeder on the link.

There are a number of different types of non-toxic leger weights now on the market, but for practical purposes I prefer to use a couple of swan shots or the Tungsten Arlesey bombs. These are weight for weight similar in size to the original lead Arlesey bombs we used to use and whilst they are far more expensive they are a worthwhile investment. For river fishing, when using weights over 1 oz, lead is still allowed in these sizes and I often flatten them slightly with a hammer to make

them hold bottom. For straight legering, some anglers prefer to use
'Risers'. These are used by carp anglers for distance fishing and their
shape makes them ideal for holding out in strong flows (see Fig. 17).

**Stuart:**  I also use the fixed paternoster for bream and roach fishing,
but I prefer to use the sliding knot for my bomb link. This allows me
to vary my length of tail at any time during a session, without having
to change my hook length (see Fig. 18). I normally use a 2 ft to 3 ft
hook length tied to the end of the main line, but the link can be slid
up or down the line at any time to increase or reduce the overall length
of tail. The knot used for this is shown in Fig. 19. When tying this,
it is important to leave the upper-most length of line to use as your link,
cutting off the lower length. This helps to prevent the knot slipping down
on the cast. The knot itself is the same as the Billy Lane sliding float
stop knot, but the length of line used is longer, to allow you sufficient
length for your link. Like Maurice, I vary this from 12 inches for stillwater
fishing to 4 or 6 inches for river fishing.

For the larger species, I use the double loop system that I also use
for river feeder fishing. Again, this acts as a bolt rig, but instead of using
an Arlesey bomb, I use a carp Zip lead (see Fig. 11). This has a thin
spigot protruding an inch or so from the top of the lead and this helps
to prevent tangles. For river fishing I also flatten these with a hammer.
For stillwater fishing, for bream and roach, I also prefer to use the Tungsten Arlesley bombs, but when the range permits and for reasons of economy, I will often use a couple of swan shots on the link instead, particularly
if the swim is snaggy. If I get caught in weeds etc, they will pull off
the line and can be replaced much quicker than having to re-tie a new
rig due to breakage.

**Maurice:**  You will notice that we keep all of these rigs as simple as
possible. This is very important. We always try to avoid the use of ironmongery such as swivels and plastic booms etc. These only provide a
focal point for the line to tangle around and collect any debris that is
coming down with the current. There is no advantage in using them with
the fine hook lengths we mainly use. Tie a length of 1½ lb or 1 lb line
to a swivel and try to make it turn by twisting the line and you will
see that it will just not work. The only way to prevent line twist with
finer lines is to take care on the retrieve and try to bring your tackle
up to the surface for as long as possible when winding back in, especially
when using a double maggot or caster on the hook. Always ensure that
you hook these baits opposite to each other so they lie pointing downwards
as opposed to outwards (see Fig. 20). This will cut down the risk of
them spinning as they are retrieved.

One type of feeder that we have not mentioned is the wire caged

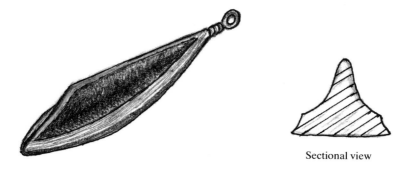

Sectional view

Fig. 17. 'Riser' leads, ideal for holding out in strong flows.

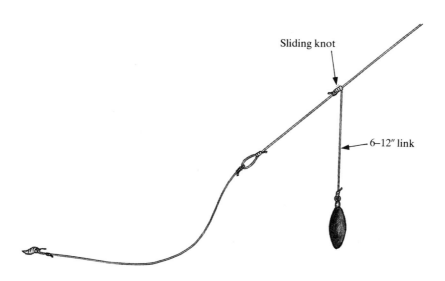

Sliding knot

6–12″ link

Fig. 18. Stuart's adjustable paternoster rig.

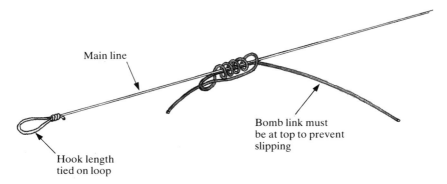

Main line

Bomb link must
be at top to prevent
slipping

Hook length
tied on loop

Fig. 19. Tying a sliding link.

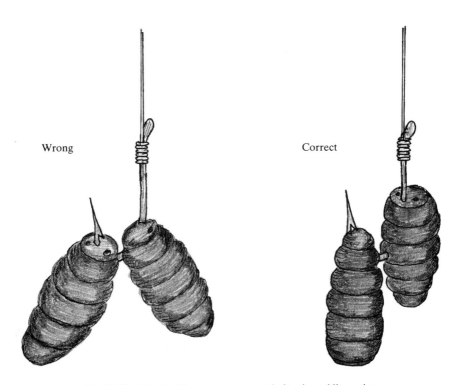

Wrong

Correct

Fig. 20. Hooking double caster to prevent bait spin and line twist.

feeder. The advantage of these is that they offer very little resistance on the retrieve due to their wire mesh construction (see Fig. 9). The only problem with them is that due to this, they tend to hug the bottom on the retrieve, as opposed to rising up as the plastic ones do. Obviously in weedy or snaggy swims this can be a big disadvantage, but if you are fishing on a clear bottom they are ideal, particularly in the smaller sizes. As long as you have a full understanding of how your tackle works under the water, you can then decide what to use with regards to the various situations you come up against.

# Legering and Feeder Fishing on Still Waters

**Q** *Let us consider legering and feeder fishing on stillwater. When you get to your peg, how do you go about assessing your swim and locating depths and features such as shelves, ledges, sand bars and weed beds etc?*

**Stuart:** It is essential to find out as much as possible about the venue beforehand, particularly if it is water you are not familiar with. This will not only influence which methods you will use, but also how much bait and ground bait you will need to take. Obviously it is no good taking just a couple of pounds of ground bait only to find when you get there, that the water contains large bream and you will need 30 lb or 40 lb of fish to stand any chance of winning. On the other hand, you do not want to be humping 2 or 3 stone of ground bait and a gallon of squatts and casters, only to find that the target species are roach and perch. By finding out the current form of a venue you have a greater idea of what to expect. By stillwaters we are also including large drains and sluice controlled rivers such as the Nene, Welland and the Huntspill.

The cost of bait these days is such that you must use it to its best advantage. Obviously you must have enough to do the job if you draw well, but on the other hand you cannot afford to waste it if you draw out of it. One advantage of us travelling to a match as a group is that, if it is a patchy venue with well-known 'Hot Spots' we can pool our bait together and distribute it after the draw to those of us who will need it. Accurate information is essential when doing this. We rely a lot on individual knowledge of local venues, or the match circuit 'grape-vine' for the more distant waters. If you fish on your own then you must take sufficient bait in case you draw a 'flyer'. Although you may draw out of it and not use it at all, you must be prepared not to waste the opportunity if it arises.

**Maurice:** Where possible of course, if the venue is strange to you, then a practice visit is always well worth the effort and expense, particularly if the match is important to you. At least you can see and get a feel of the venue and by talking to local anglers or visiting the local tackle shop you can obtain a lot of information as to its nature and current form. On the big bream venues the shoals tend to move about during the course of the season and what are no hope pegs one month, can be 'flyers' another. So it is important that any information is bang up to date. Sometimes the information you get can be unintentionally misleading and by going and sussing it out for yourelf, you can set trends rather than slavishly follow them.

We always try to fish venues that we know well. We do not go to distant, unknown venues unless we have to. But with the Summer League Knockout Matches, we can find ourselves on any number of strange venues and we are only allowed, as a team, one practice session and on occasions due to other commitments, we cannot always take advantage of those. In these circumstances we often have to keep a close eye on the opposition and try to suss out what they are doing.

Once you have reached your peg you must then find out the exact geography of the swim. I normally attach a large lead, say three-quarters of an ounce, to my line and make a number of exploratory casts at different distances and in different areas within the confines of my swim, to find any changes in depths and assess the nature of the bottom. By counting the drop from when my bomb hits the surface to when the tip falls back, I can judge what depths I have in front of me and the whereabouts of any bars or ledges. Also by winding back slowly, allowing the bomb to drag along the bottom, I can locate any weed beds or snags. This is very important. Many anglers make the mistake of putting in their ground bait first, only to find they have put it into the middle of an underwater weed bed or in an area that is full of snags. It is important to find clean areas between weed beds that are relatively snag-free. Also it is possible to fire out ground bait further than you are able to reach with the equipment you have brought with you.

If you have a variation in depths, you need to assess with regards to the prevailing conditions, where you think the fish are likely to be.

In warm temperatures, particularly after a cold spell, the fish are more likely to be in the shallower areas. In cold conditions they will probably be in the deeper areas. The time of day will also influence this decision. In most cases, providing the different areas are reasonably well apart, it can pay you to bait up both areas and alternate fishing in them until you find where they are. We normally bait up and feed several different lines even in waters that are relatively uniform in depth and features, particularly if they contain a variety of match winning species. On an out and out bream or carp venue then under these circumstances we would concentrate our efforts more to just one particular area.

**Stuart:**  I also follow the same routine as Maurice. We just do it automati-

Fig. 21. Correctly positioning and supporting a quivertip rod on stillwater.

cally on every venue, even the ones that we know intimately. The other important consideration is making sure your equipment is laid out properly and your seat box is stable. All our boxes are fitted with adjustable feet to enable us to counter an unevenness of the bank. It is important when you need to concentrate on a quivertip for 5 hours that you are comfortable. Once your seat is correctly positioned, you must then position your rod rests so that your rod is stable and the tip is as close as possible to the surface of the water in windy conditions. Sometimes you may need to shield the tip from the worst effects of the wind with your umbrella in very exposed situations. This is a far more important consideration than your personal comfort. Also make sure that you can see your quivertip properly. Always point it away from the direction of the sun. On stillwater you can position your rod either side of you, so it's pointless positioning it with the sun shining in your eyes or its reflection in the water dazzling you. Although I do not use them, some anglers like to use a target board to help them pick out those small indications when conditions are hard, or to shield the tip from the worst effects of the wind (see Fig. 24). You also need to ensure that the line enters the water cleanly and cannot get caught up on any underwater obstructions such as weeds, lilies or reed beds, and the area behind you, where

Fig. 22. Stuart demonstrating correct feeder casting techniques.

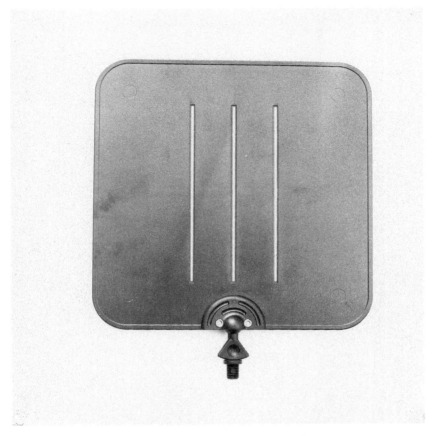

Fig. 23. A modern commercial target board.

your hook length will be when you cast, is also free of obstructions. There is nothing more frustrating than being caught up and cracking off on the cast. Always clear any weeds or obstructions from behind you to prevent this. Also ensure that the rod tip is also unobstructed to allow you to draw the rod back cleanly on the strike.

Whilst on the subject of striking, it is very rare these days with modern quivertips that you need to strike hard. Normally a smooth lifting of the rod is all that is needed to connect with the fish. Often, with the very fine hook lengths we use, this would only result in cracking off anyway. Always make sure, where possible, that your keep net is positioned within easy reach without you having to move off your basket

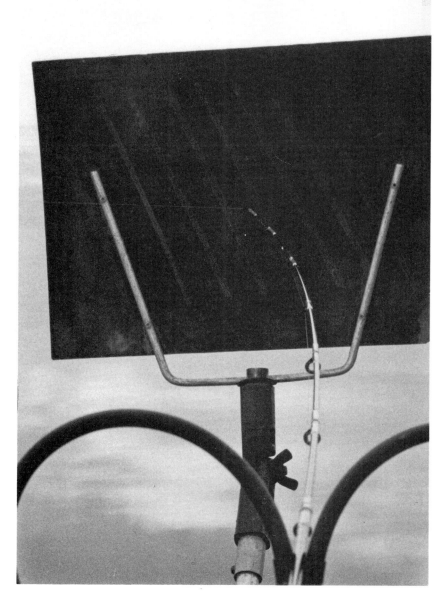

Fig. 24. Positioning of quiver tip using a target board.

to put in a fish. Also put your landing net next to you for the same reasons. Ground bait bowls, bait containers and tackle trays with spare hooks, lines and feeders should also be within easy reach. When using a swim feeder it is much easier to have your bait or ground bait mix either in a tray attached to the front of your box or to wear a bait apron. This saves a lot of time during the course of a match when loading your feeder.

**Maurice:**  Talking about being comfortable, I've made myself a platform with adjustable legs on it. It's very useful when you are fishing in margins where you would like to sit down but you are stood in 18 inches of water. I can put the platform down, sit my box on the top, clear of the water surface, and get myself comfortable and concentrate on my fishing. It also comes in handy when you are pegged on rush beds etc. You do not have the problem of your box wobbling about spoiling your concentration. On places like Eckington and on the lower Avon, it is essential. On those matches 95% of the anglers fish sitting down. It is that type of venue, where you need to keep low or the fish will be spooked. The problem is that due to the rushes and the wide margins, a conventional box, even with adjustable legs, will not reach down far enough to sit stable. The banks are also very steep, so it is impossible to sit on your box up there. Although I have made my own, good lightweight versions are available commercially, though most anglers buy them for pole fishing. But they are good for all types of fishing and if you visit a number of venues with similar conditions to those I have outlined, they are a worthwhile investment.

**Q**  *What are your initial opening tactics with regards to rigs, tail lengths and feeding? Does the swing tip still have a role to play or have you now gone over completely to the use of the quivertip?*

**Stuart:**  If I were bream fishing, I would always start off with an open-ended feeder or straight lead and ground bait tactics. I would have a 4 ft hook length initially and if I were using worm and caster, a size 18 or preferably a size 16 hook. The hook length would be a 1 ½ lb breaking strain for openers. If I thought the water would stand it, I would initially put in up to 20 balls of feed. This may seem excessive to some people, but if I thought I had drawn well and the fish would feed well, I would be fishing for a win. It may take an hour for things to settle down, but then if they move in I know I would have enough bait there to hold them.

On waters where this sort of opening gambit was too risky, I would cast about 10 feederfuls of squatts or casters, plugged either end with just enough ground bait to hold them in on the cast. I would do this

Fig. 25. Rod rest heads used when legering.

without even tying on a hook length at this stage, the object being to lay a carpet of loose feed in the shortest possible time. I would then revert to the straight lead or continue with the feeder if I think the fish will stand it.

We never go into a match like this blind. We will always ring around to find out the current form and, where possible, practice a few days before the match, each of us using a different approach to assess which method is likely to work on the day. We don't always get it right, that is the nature of bream fishing, but when we do, then providing we get the draw we are in with a good chance. As I have said, if you know the match is going to be won with 30 lb or 40 lb of bream then an odd feederful is not going to get you that sort of weight. But if it seems like it's going to be a hard 15 lb day, then these are the tactics to adopt. Only experience can teach you which approach to use, but you must fish to win and take enough bait in case you need it. This may seem an obvious statement to make, but it's surprising how many people who fish these types of matches do not realise just what is involved and many a match winning opportunity has been lost due to not having enough bait to hold the fish; a classic example of false economy. At the other extreme, you also get anglers who, unlike ourselves, do not do their homework and fill it in regardless of conditions. If you draw next to one of these on a bad day then you just have to resign yourself to having to struggle.

**Maurice:** Whilst we like fishing these types of venues as individuals, we dread them when fishing as a team, particularly if there are not many back-up species, such as roach, perch or skimmers. When team fishing on bream waters, unless we are 100% certain they will take plenty of feed, we would always err on the side of caution, opening our match on the feeder, particularly if we feel we have drawn out of the bream areas. In this case we will only put 2 or 3 feederfuls out, switching to the straight lead in the hope of picking up a few roach or whatever other species may be going. Whilst bream will often take a lot of feed, other species will not and the last thing you want to do in a team event, particularly if it's fished on a points basis, is to feed off the other species.

Often under these circumstances we will start off by using a Sigma Wand in conjunction with 1 lb or 12 oz hook lengths and maggot or caster on a size 20 or 22 hook. When using these finer hook lengths we will always use the longest tail length possible to allow plenty of stretch to cushion the strike and prevent cracking off or pulling out. I often start off by using a tail of up to 6 ft long, shortening it if I get stretched or sucked maggots without seeing any indication on the tip. When using these long tails it is important to straighten the tail after casting. If the tail is left to fall in a heap and is not straightened out, bites will not be indicated. When using a straight leger rig this is achieved by over-casting the baited area and winding back over it. When using a feeder you must, of course, cast to the baited area and then straighten the tail out by pulling it over the feed after it has emptied. During the summer months we will always be working our bait, continually lifting or twitching back through the baited area to try to induce a bite. This is always assuming, of course, that the bottom is relatively clean and we are not pulling our terminal tackle into weed. If the bottom is completely covered in weed, then we will always use a floating caster or maggot to ensure it lies on the top of the weed, but will have to leave it alone after the cast. Try twitching it under these circumstances and you will pull it into the weed. This is why it is so important to establish the nature of the bottom at the beginning and to try where possible to find a clear area.

When casting, it is important to select a marker on the far bank and cast to this. This will help you to keep the bait concentrated into the area you have chosen to fish. Accurate casting is essential and you must practice this. You need to face the marker holding the rod above your head and, keeping your eyes on where you want to cast, bringing the rod smoothly forwards. If the bomb or feeder goes to the left or the right then your action is wrong. Always keep your head and body straight. Never cast from the side by twisting your body. This is completely wrong, and you will never cast well consistently. Also by turning and looking at the bomb as you cast, you will be unable to follow it properly (see Fig. 22).

Do not worry if you are a couple of feet either side of the baited area. At long range it is almost impossible to land it in the same spot time after time. In fact this can more often than not be beneficial. I never like to take fish from the middle of the baited area. I always prefer to pick them off from around the edge of the shoal, just like a snooker player prefers to pick off the loose reds from around the pack first. Like the snooker player, I never go into the main pack until I have exhausted the supply of loose fish. The last thing you want to do is hook a fish from the middle of the shoal. This will unsettle the fish and you will probably lose them. I always try to feed on an area of several square yards in a diamond pattern (see Fig. 26). The corners of the diamond are marked A, B, C, D. I will always try to alternate my casts around the areas marked B, C & D avoiding the centre of the diamond and area A. I would only cast into this area if bites completely cease. This is to try to establish whether the fish are still there or not. If they are, I will get line bites as I will have cast my bomb just beyond point A, with my line passing through the centre of the baited area. If no line bites are forthcoming I will wind back and re-bait the area, knowing that the fall off in bites is because the fish have probably moved away.

If line bites are forthcoming I know the fish are still there and I then have the difficult decision as to whether or not to feed on top of them to encourage them to start feeding again. Having established that the fish are still there, I will not cast there again until the later stages of the match or until bites have dried up, not wanting to risk hooking one from the far side of the shoal and scattering them by playing it through the middle of them.

**Stuart:** Maurice has covered the basic feeding tactics well, but it is important to stress that bream fishing is a waiting game. It is very seldom that you will catch straight away and many a match has been won with most of the fish being taken in the last hour or so. It is also important to sit on your hands when the fish do move in. If you start striking at every little movement of the tip you will miss a lot of bites and unsettle the fish. You must let the bite develop. Often you will get the initial touch, then a slightly more positive pull followed by a dig-dig-dig of

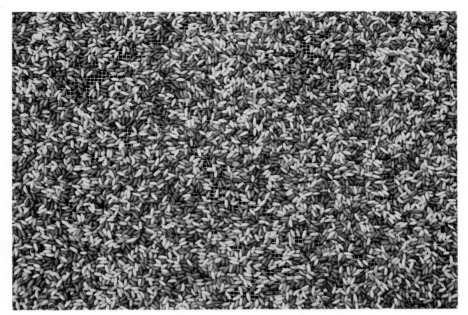

Fresh casters: on the right day, the deadliest of all baits.

Squatts: an essential bait for bream fishing.

Maurice's 24-13 match-winning weight of chub, caught using feeder tactics on the Warwick-shire Avon at Twyford Farm.

A sample of the continental groundbaits now very much in favour.

Stuart feeder-fishing on a local stillwater venue. Note the efficient tackle layout.

Releasing the clips at the bottom of the Steadfast Protectanet.

Fish being released out of bottom of net into the weighing net.

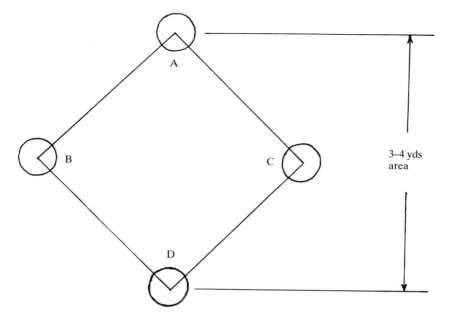

Fig. 26. Groundbaiting pattern.

the tip. You must then wait until the tip goes right round and stays there. All you need to do then is just gently lift into the fish and it will be on. If your tip suddenly pulls round with no preliminary indications and when you lift the rod there is nothing there, then this will have been a line bite. You must then gently retrieve the tackle so as not to frighten the fish, check the bait to confirm that it has not been touched and re-cast, but not quite as far. The fact that you have had a line bite means that the fish are between you and your previous position, so you need to cast shorter or to one side of that area.

Some days you may not get the tip pulled right around. If you get the preliminary knocks but the bite does not develop and the bait has been completely sucked, you may need to shorten your tail. If the tip still does not go right round this may be because the fish are feeding so well and the shoal is so tightly packed, that the fish are not moving off with the bait. You must then experiment with your striking to establish which of the various tip readings you are getting means that a fish is on. Again, a smooth lift as opposed to a fierce sweep is preferable.

Often when you know fish are there but they are not taking the bait on the bottom, you can often get bites on the drop by lengthening your tail and using more buoyant baits such as a floating caster or a semi-floating gozzer. It is also very important, as I have mentioned in the chapter on baits, to keep ringing the changes between the various baits to keep the bites coming. This is why I prefer to use a sliding paternoster as opposed to a fixed paternoster. It allows me to instantly vary the length of my tail, to keep in touch with the way the fish are feeding. With regards to which types of tip I use, these days I nearly always use the quivertip. The development of these as bite indicators has come on a long way since the early days. Now with modern materials they are much finer and more sensitive than ever before. Having said that, I love to use the swingtip. It is a superb method of fishing, especially when it's a sit on your hands situation. The thrill experienced when that tip swings up and holds is tremendous, the problem is that it is very difficult to cast at long range accurately. Also, most modern leger rods are designed as quivertip rods and do not have the facility for using them with a swingtip, so I don't use it in match situations.

If I fished a lot on the fens, on rivers like the Nene and Welland I possibly would use it more, but ours is not a swingtip area.

**Maurice:** I never use a swingtip these days, but I would not deter anyone from using one on suitable venues. Top bream anglers like Ivan Marks and Tom Bedder have made it an art. They can cast at any range with a swingtip and never experience the problem of the tip wrapping around the rod end as many anglers do, so if anyone can master its use half as good as these lads, they should do well with it. But as Stuart has said, now with the development of modern quivertips such as those used on the Sigma Wand, its use is not as essential as it used to be. You can virtually tie modern quivertips in a knot, they are that soft and strong, so I find that they cover all of my legering requirements.

We have discussed bream fishing tactics on stillwaters and I feel we have covered most of the relevant points. Roach fishing on the other hand is a different ball game altogether. Unless I am caster fishing, most of my roach fishing is done by using block-end feeders or, if I can feed comfortably with the catapult at the required range, the straight lead. Again the paternoster is the preferred rig to use in conjunction with 1 lb hook lengths and small fine wire hooks. The size of feeders used will be much smaller than when bream fishing. The cut down Drennan feeder links are my normal choice, used in conjunction with the rubber sleeve (see Fig. 10).

When caster fishing outside catapult range I will feed the casters and, during the summer months, caster and hemp, in a small open-ended feeder. I will put it in the feeder neat with just a small plug of ground bait mixed very dry to hold it in on the cast. I often use a block-end feeder with the lower cap removed so it is only open at one end (see Fig. 27). This allows for the minimum use of ground bait. This same

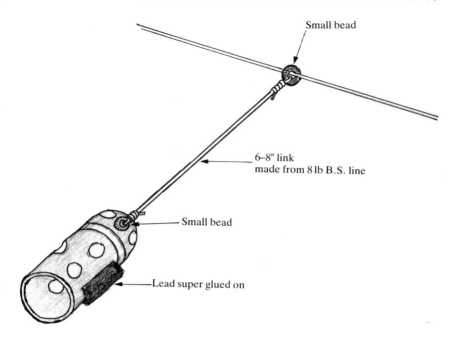

Small bead

6–8″ link
made from 8 lb B.S. line

Small bead

Lead super glued on

Fig. 27. Maurice's 'open ended' feeder used for bream fishing on the Gloucester Canal. Loose cap removed and end filled with a pinch of groundbait to hold in feed during cast.

method is also used when chub or skimmer fishing on the Gloucester Canal, in conjunction with casters or squatts.

As with bream, I will normally start off with a 4 ft tail. If I am getting bites but not seeing any indication of the tip, I will shorten off until I start to connect with the fish. If I am getting plenty of bites and fish on the 4 ft tail, I will also shorten off to speed up the process and improve the indication, providing that the catch rate is maintained. I will also increase the hook size under these conditions to minimise the risk of dropping fish off, and to speed up the playing time. I will also increase the strength of the hook length, if I can get away with it. It is pointless under these circumstances using small hooks on fine bottoms if they will take, say, a single or double maggot on an 18 or 16 tied to a 1½ lb or 2 lb bottom.

If, on the other hand, it is a hard day and I need to use a 22 or 24 hook on a 12 oz tail I will do, if that is the only way I can get bites.

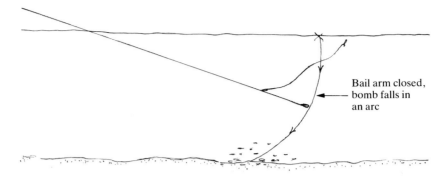

Fig. 28. When straight legering bomb can be cast beyond baited area and bail arm closed whilst bomb is falling. Bait can be twitched through the baited area.

I may also have to increase my tail length to 6 ft under these conditions, providing I can see the bites.

When using a straight lead over loose feed I will normally over-cast the baited area, engaging the pick up as the bomb hits the surface and working the bait through the swim by twitching or lifting the rig back at regular intervals, a few inches at a time. Roach love to take a moving bait like this, as opposed to one just left on the bottom. You are also covering a greater area of the swim taking the bait to the fish, as opposed to waiting for the fish to find the bait. It is amazing how many anglers just cast in and leave the bait in one place and at the end of the day moan that they have only caught a fraction of your weight and how they wish they had drawn your peg. Often they are on a better peg with a greater potential than mine, but they just do not fish it properly and maximise its potential.

When feeder fishing, particularly on deeper waters, you need to leave the bail arm open when the feeder hits the surface, allowing it to go straight down, as opposed to falling in an arc as when you are using the straight lead (see Fig. 28). When the feeder hits the bottom, and after giving it sufficient time to empty in the case of a block-end, you then lift it forwards to straighten the tail and to draw the hook bait over the feed (see Fig. 29).

It is also important to leave the bail arm open until the feeder or bomb has settled when fishing close to the far bank or against reed beds etc. Obviously, you want to get the bait as close to these features as possible. In windy conditions you would put the rod tip under the surface whilst the bomb is falling so that the line does not bow.

When long range feeder fishing, because your feed is concentrated

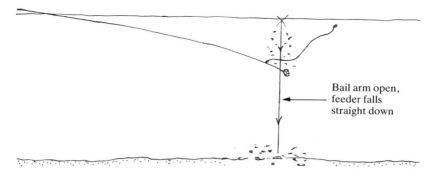

Fig. 29. When feeder fishing, bail arm must be left open to allow feeder to fall straight down with the feed. Once settled, tail can be pulled over the feed.

in a much smaller area, you may not be able to work it quite so often or over the same sort of distance in the early stages of a match, as you can when straight legering over catapulted feed. But, later on, when you have spread the feed around a bit by the natural variations in your casting accuracy, you can work the bait through much more. During periods of low water temperatures or on other occasions when bites are few and far between, after laying your initial carpet of feed with your feeder, it can pay under these circumstances to switch to the straight leger until bites are forthcoming, then alternate between this and the feeder to adjust your feeding rate to suit the response.

I always, where possible, fish and feed several different lines at various ranges when roach fishing, sometimes using different baits on different lines. I will always have a loose fed line at closer range and a feeder line at long range, alternating these as and when it is necessary. This allows me to rest a swim and allows the fish to regain their confidence and settle down again. This is an obvious point, but one which is often over-looked by many anglers. We would not do this so much when bream fishing because of the need to concentrate the shoal, but it does work well when fishing for roach.

**Q** *How do you cope with extreme conditions such as strong winds and undertow? What changes would you make to your basic approach during cold conditions and low water temperatures?*

**Stuart:** On some days when you literally have waves breaking on the shore of the lake, normal bite indication is out of the question. Under these conditions I would use a larger lead on the double loop river rig, wind down to it after casting and fish for drop back bites. You are virtually using the carp anglers bolt rig tactics and hoping that any fish that do have a go will hook themselves. In strong, as opposed to storm force winds, you need to get your tip as close to the surface of the water as possible, actually putting it right under the water once your bomb or feeder hits the surface, to ensure that the line is pulled under by the falling weight before it can be allowed to bow on the surface. Once it is sunk you put the rod on its rest. You will also need a bit of extra lead on to give you something to pull against and again to keep your line tight and to sink it well below the surface. You can protect your tip from the worst of the wind by putting your brolly in the water to shield it, providing, of course, that the margin is reasonably shallow. On these occasions you would use a fast sinking line such as Maxima or Shakespeare Alpha. These are dark coloured lines that can be relied upon to sink quickly. On really hard cold days where bites are few or far between I would go smaller in the hook but sometimes go up to a 1½ lb or 1.7 lb hook length so that when I do get the bite I will not crack off. Even anglers with our experience can get excited at getting our first bite for 3 hours, make a grab, and bang, it's gone! I often feel that hook size, rather than line thickness, is the more important consideration, within reasonable limits of course, when fish are feeding on a still bait nailed down on the bottom.

If things are really hard and I know I need more than just a few bits to do any good in the match, then providing it is an individual event and I know that there are bigger fish in the water, I will go to the other extreme and fish a big bait such as worm or bread flake on a big hook, in the hope of connecting with one of these. After all, what have you to lose? You will not win the match with a few bits, especially if someone already has a bream or whatever in the net, but you just may come from behind if one of the big fish does have a go. This catch 22 situation applies to all sorts of venues and situations, except, of course, in team matches fished on a points system.

**Maurice:** I don't add much to what Stuart has said on this. Under these cold conditions, I have on occasions gone down to 12 oz bottoms on the leger, but if I do have to do this I can safely say I am not going to win anything. Usually, if I do go to this extreme, it is during a team match when I am scratching around for points. Under normal conditions I never like to go below a 1 lb hook length, especially if there is the chance of a bigger fish such as a bream.

You will need to cut right back on your feed during low water temperatures. At long range you will use a very small feeder that will only take about a dozen maggots. After a few casts with this, without getting a response, I would then switch to a straight leger, twitching the bait back through the baited area, but without introducing any further feed until I start to get bites.

During periods of strong winds, the fish can, on occasions, feed better than in what we would consider to be more ideal conditions. There are times when a good blow is needed on a stillwater to stir things up and get the water circulating; it is the stillwater equivalent of a flood on a river. Under these circumstances, I am always happier if I am pegged on the windward bank with the wind blowing in my face. This is the area where the fish are most likely to be feeding under these conditions.

**Q** *How appropriate are leger and swimfeeder methods to canal fishing? When do they give you an advantage over the pole and float methods generally associated with these types of waters?*

**Maurice:** There are canals, and there are canals! By this I mean that we are looking at the extremes between the narrow, shallow canals such as the Grand Union etc, or the wide deep canals such as the Gloucester, which is built to take ocean-going cargo ships. In between these extremes are the medium size canals you have in Yorkshire, such as the Aire and Calder and the Stainforth and Keadby and New Junction canals.

Taking the smaller Midlands canals first, it is very seldom that you would use feeder tactics on these waters, although straight legering with the Wand is sometimes used in very windy conditions, when it is impossible to present the bait properly on the pole, or the float. Bait presentation and range are the main considerations when deciding where to use legering methods. Obviously range does not come into it on these narrow canals, but on occasions legering may be the only means of presenting your bait properly under certain conditions. The reason you would not use a swimfeeder is that due to the distances involved, you can always introduce your feed by hand or by catapult under all but the most extreme of conditions. I would normally use a straight paternoster rig with a couple of AAA or a swan shots or a small Arlesey bomb on the link and a fine 1 lb or 12 oz hook length (see Fig. 16). Personally, I always use my Sigma Wand for canal fishing, but I know some people who specialise on these sorts of venues, do use these tiny 6 ft Wands in these situations.

The tactics do not vary much. In the summer months, the target area is generally the far ledge for skimmers and chub, coming down the shelf into the deep water during colder conditions or when after bream and roach (see Fig. 30).

On the medium size and large canals, leger tactics and mini feeder tactics will be used on a far more regular basis, and often is 'the' method, particularly when the target species are bream and chub. Many of these venues are now very popular match venues with a good head of chub patrolling up and down the far bank. These are good sized fish and a

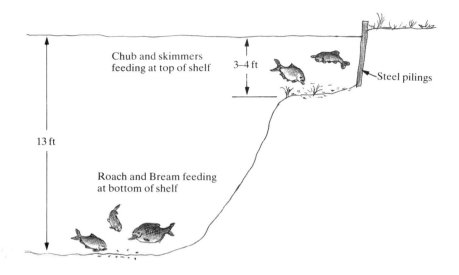

Fig. 30. Position of fish on far bank of Gloucester Canal.

dozen or so of these can often be a match winner. Bream and roach are also a target species during the summer months, though small gudgeon can be a nuisance once you move off the ledge into the main channel. The methods and species in these canals are very similar to those we use on the Gloucester Canal.

**Stuart::**   When we fish the Gloucester Canal, the leger is, as Maurice has said, 'the' method. We normally set up a couple of Wands, one with the mini feeders shown in Fig. 10, and a straight leger rod. If the wind is bad it is no use trying to feed over the far side with the catapult as the feed just gets blown everywhere, so what we do is plop the feeder over a couple of times and then go in with the straight lead. If using squatts or casters we use the little open-ended feeder or the single-ended feeder with the minimum of ground bait needed to hold the feed in on the cast. If using maggots we do, of course, use the little block-end feeders that only take a dozen or so maggots. In the summer months squatts, casters and gozzers are the main feed and hook baits. In the winter we use red or bronze maggots. We use a tail about 4 ft long and this will be normally a 1 lb breaking strain. During the warmer weather we concentrate on the far ledge, fishing the top of this as close to the far bank as is possible. Here we are hoping to connect with chub and skimmers. When the temperatures are lower we still cast across to the top of the ledge in the hope of catching a bonus chub on the drop, but once the tail has settled we inch the bomb back until it falls down over the lip of the ledge. You know when this happens. The tip pulls round, and it seems as if your bomb has fallen over the edge of the world with the time it takes for it to hit the bottom and the tip to straighten again. You are now fishing in roach territory, although during cold spells you will also catch skimmers there as well. Again, you would feed with a couple of feederfuls and then switch back to the straight leger until you start to get bites and you think that they will need a little bit more feed. The worst thing you can do on any canal, even on a big water like the Gloucester, is to over-feed the swim. Once you have done this it is seldom that you will be able to rectify the situation.

**Maurice:** Another species which is very popular on canals in the summer months is tench. Again, these can respond well to leger tactics and careful feeding. I remember fishing the Newry Canal in Ireland. Everyone was legering for these tench. Carp are also a popular target species on some canals and in recent years many of the smaller canals have been stocked with this species. The biggest problem on any canals, especially during the summer months, is boat traffic, and this causes all sorts of problems to your fishing and feeding. Many boaters think they are doing you a favour by going down the far side, not realising that this is where most match anglers will be fishing and feeding. Sometimes they can bring a dead swim back to life, but more often than not they will kill it for you.

Generally, the important rule is, not to feed when the canal is pulling due to boat traffic and lock gates etc. If you feel that the occasional small ball of cloud bait and squatts or casters may be helpful, drop it in behind a passing boat, right into its wash, but only if the fish are responding well and you know that there are plenty of them. This method usually only applies when bream fishing.

Please remember — litter loses fishing

# Legering and Feeder Fishing on Flowing Waters

**Q** *Let us move onto legering and feeder fishing on rivers. When you get to your peg, how do you go about assessing the swim? What procedure do you adopt in selecting and trimming your rigs to suit the flow and conditions?*

**Maurice:** Again, much depends upon the species you are after and the time of the year. You know by experience or local knowledge which species are present, or if it is a new venue, you will ring round or visit the water to get the latest up-to-date informtion. During the summer months on rivers with plenty of natural features such as over-hanging trees, rush beds and fast gravel bottomed runs, you would fish to these various features, depending upon the target species. On rivers such as the Warwickshire Avon, the Thames, the Bristol Avon and parts of the Severn, the target species will be chub and these will be mainly found over the far side of the river particularly where natural fish holding features such as over-hanging trees, bays and rush beds are to be found. On parts of the Severn and the Thames these may be as far as 50 or 60 yards across, so the longer converted float rods are normally employed to reach these areas and keep as much line off of the water as possible. On the narrower rivers the more conventional light to medium feeder rods would be used, depending upon the flow. In the winter months when the rivers may be carrying a bit of extra water, any far bank features such as bays where fish can shelter away from the main current will be obvious target areas if you are fortunte to draw opposite them.

In the summer months when the target may be barbel, you will fish the streamy areas of the river where there is the fastest flow, providing the river bed is suitable. The favourite spots for barbel are over gravel beds and these are normally found where the current is the strongest.

The deeper, slower areas of the river are the normal holding areas for bream, where they are present, and if you know that the area you are drawn in can produce a match winning weight of these fish, then these will be your target species.

Often on rivers like the Warwickshire Avon, you can draw areas where both bream and chub are present. In these situations you will feed two lines, the far bank for chub and the deeper areas in mid-river for bream, alternating in respose to the fish.

On broad, featureless rivers, such as the Trent, fish location is more difficult. The fish tend to be far more widespread and chub can often be caught in mid-river. There is also a much wider variety of species, all competing in the same areas for food. Some areas, particularly the shallower swims do contain more chub than the deeper slower stretches, where bream and skimmers are the dominant species. The river is also full of big roach, but these do not seem to show as much in the summer when using leger or feeder tactics. On the lower parts of the Trent below Nottingham, I normally fish one line in mid-river with the feeder and loose feed on a closer line to come back onto later on in the match. This line will normally be fished with the straight leger. I do tend to use larger feeders on this part of the trent to what I would use in the upper-reaches or on the Warwickshire Avon. Most of my chub fishing and in fact my general river fishing is done on the block-end, using bronze maggots. There are occasions when bream fishing, where I will use caster and ground bait tactics, but in recent seasons these are few and far between. Again, knowledge of the current form of the venue is important in deciding which baits to use.

If I were fishing for barbel on the River Severn then it has to be caster and hemp as things stand at the moment, but who knows what will be the most effective method in the new season? On local venues we are always trying to find new and more effective methods, but whilst the established methods continue to produce the goods, then these are the ones that must be used.

With regard to rigs, I still prefer to use the running leger with the feeder (see Fig. 7). When using the straight leger, I will also use the running leger with a bomb instead of a feeder.

The weight of the feeder used needs to be trimmed so that it will just hold position in the flow where you intend to fish, with experience you can normally judge to within a ¼ oz or so the size you will need. This is where we come to the complicated bit. As well as deciding the *weight* of the feeder, you will also need to consider its *size*, or to be more precise its *volume*. This is where many anglers go wrong. Because they may need to use a heavy feeder, they automatically assume that this means a bigger feeder. To some extent their thinking on this is conditioned by the manufacturers who make heavier feeders larger than the lighter ones. As the feeders step up in weight, they also increase in size. This is wrong. On many occasions, particularly when chub fishing, you will want a large volume feeder initially to get the fish to feed, but to maintain the catch rate you will often have to reduce the capacity of the feeder with regards to the volume of the feed being introduced. But of course, as you are still fishing on the same line, you still need the same weight to hold position.

As we go through this chapter, when we refer to the size of a feeder we will be meaning its volume. When we refer to its weight we will mean the amount of lead attached to it. I have some feeders in my box that only hold a dozen or so maggots, but may carry 1 oz or 1½ oz of lead. These cannot be bought commercially but they can be made by adding on the clip-on leads that are now availble in most tackle shops (see Fig. 13). On the really small ones, I may stick extra strips of lead onto the sides with Superglue, with one strip stuck on top of another. Sometimes when using the smaller feeders you do not need quite so much lead to hold out in the same spot, due to the less resistance of the reduced area of plastic against the current.

Once you have selected your 'size' of feeder you then need to trim it to suit the conditions. What I normally do is to cast the feeder slightly up-stream and peel a few feet of line off of the reel to produce a bow. I then close the bail arm and put the rod on the rest. If the feeder continues to move down the swim I will add lead to it, or select a heavier feeder of the same size. If I cast in and it holds straight away I will then need to reduce the weight slightly. It is essential for the method to work, that the feeder just holds bottom in front of you, so that when a fish takes the bait, the feeder will move causing the rod tip to fall back. This is what is called a 'drop back' bite and we would be looking to 90% of our bites being drop backs when feeder fishing for chub or bream on flowing water. The bow I have mentioned also plays an essential part in making this method work. If you just tighten up to the feeder without allowing this bow to form you may get cracked off, it really is the 'key' to the method.

**Stuart:**  I trim my feeders much the same as Maurice. Sometimes when you are trimming them you think you have got it right, but the feeder may be held by a ledge or a small snag instead of by its own weight. One way of checking this is to gently pull six inches or so of line from the butt ring and if the feeder moves and then holds again you know it is clear and is properly trimmed. If you need to pull really hard to move it you then know that it is either too heavy or it was caught up. You then need to try it in another part of the swim but on the same line to establish which is which.

I always remember when I fished a winter match on the Avon. Dave Harrell warned me not to go too near to the far bank because under the water was the remains of a rush bed which had died off during the winter. He told me that if I got too far across I would be into these rushes. To establish where the rush beds finished and the clean bottom began I had to use this method to make sure that the feeder was clear and could be moved by the fish when I had a bite. I always use the double loop method (shown in Fig. 12) when feeder fishing, for the reasons I have mentioned in the chapter on rigs. When using the straight leger on rivers I prefer to use the running link leger.

Like Maurice, most of my feeder fishing on rivers is done with the block-end feeder and maggots. On some venues you may need to use caster, but I would normally still use a block-end, allowing the current to wash the casters out of the feeder. They do seem to empty just as quickly as maggots, though I must stress that this only happens on flowing water. On a bream venue we will use ground bait and casters in an open-ended feeder if we are certain that the method is suited to the venue and the fish will respond. There are some venues where we use feeders the size of jam jars, but these are the exception rather than the rule. Again local knowledge and pre-match planning are the key to how you approach any particular match or venue. Some of the methods we will be discussing are peculiar to just a few particular waters and we may only use them once or twice in a season. We carry certain types of feeders and other types of equipment around with us which we may never use for ages, but they are always there for those rare occasions that we may need them.

Different areas of the country do use different methods to what we usually use in our area, but we need to know about them for those occasions when we have to fish them, such as in a National Championship. The important thing is to keep it as simple as possible, and until you have had a lot of experience of different venues, try to concentrate on matches in your own area and fully master the techniques used.

**Q** *Most anglers these days fish flowing water with the rod supported high in the air, keeping as much line out of the water as possible. How do you usually position your rods when feeder fishing and what position do you adopt when strong winds make bite indication difficult?*

**Stuart:** That method that Maurice mentioned earlier on about pointing the rod down stream and allowing that bow to form in the line, is normally the best method of all. The rod is supported high in the air, and is positioned so that it is pointing down-stream at 45° to the bank, mid-way between the bank and the feeder (see Fig. 31). You always cast a yard or so up-stream so that the feeder settles directly in front of you. You then need to peel a couple of feet of line off of the reel to form the bow. As we have previously mentioned, most of the bites will be drop backs except when barbel fishing. Then the tip will just crash round and you must be quick to allow the fish to take line and prevent being cracked off. This is why we always fish with the anti-reverse lever in the 'off' position.

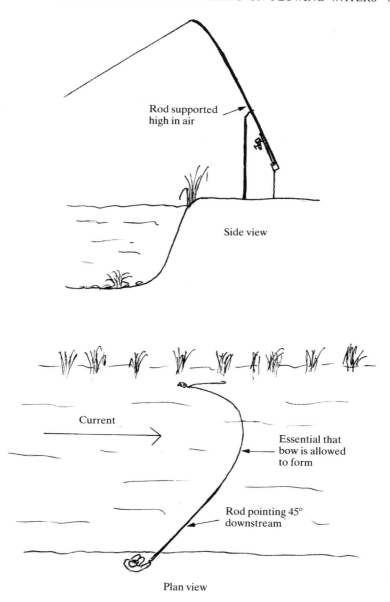

Fig. 31. Rod position when feeder fishing in flowing water.

**Maurice:** It is very rare that we ever fish a feeder down-stream of us. If we feel that the fish have moved down-stream and we need to go down after them we will always fish a straight lead on the running leger. In these circumstances the rod is pointed up-stream at 45° if fishing well across, or straight out if fishing closer in down the side. (See Fig. 32). The rod is supported parallel to the surface of the water as opposed to up in the air, as when feeder fishing. When fishing down the side with the rod pointing straight out, you have to fish a tight line, but if you are fishing across the river with the rod pointing slightly up-stream, you would still peel off a few feet of line to allow the bow to form (see Fig: 32).

This is very important when chub or barbel fishing, if you are not to get cracked off when the fish takes. I remember in the early days when we were just learning how to fish for barbel on luncheon meat, despite the use of heavy 5lb or 6lb hook lengths, we were continually being broken off by the fish taking the bait and hitting the rod tip. Eventually by trail and error we ended up by using softer rods and longer tails and allowing this bow to form down-stream. These helped to cushion the fierceness of the bite and allowed us to pick up the rod and give the fish line before it snapped us.

Anglers are still under the illusion that you need to strike at bites when legering. With modern equipment and techniques, I can honestly say that 90% of all my fish hook themselves. All you need to do is to lift the rod and they are on. With regards to reading the bites in windy conditions, when the wind is really strong you can on occasions get away by lowering the rod tip whilst feeder fishing, and if, due to the pressure of more line being in the water, the feeder will not hold, you increase the weight until it will. You will still be looking for drop-back bites, which will still be easy to see, even in strong winds, although the odd few pull bites will not be so easy to detect unless you are fishing for barbel. With regards to using the straight lead, unless you are able to shield the tip at all, if the wind is blowing really strongly down or up-stream, bite indication will be very difficult to spot when fishing for the smaller species. Under these conditions you may have to fish the rod feeder style, rigging it to indicate drop-back bites.

**Q** *What changes can you make to overcome the problems associated with the feeding habits of the various species and start to hit those un-hittable bites that plague us all from time to time? What tactics can you employ to induce bites when they are not readily forthcoming?*

**Maurice:** Those un-hittable bites especially when they are being caused by small fish such as skimmers and roach, are generally un-hittable anyway. There are a few things you can do to try to connect with them.

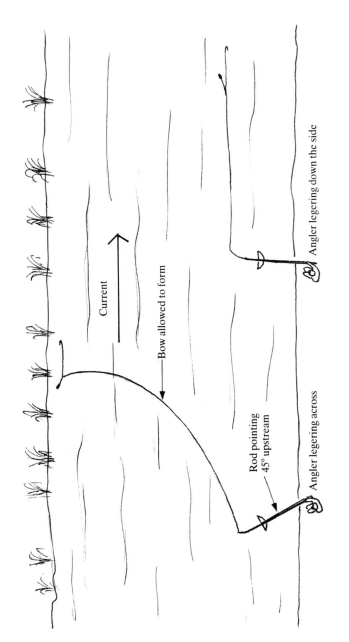

Current

Bow allowed to form

Rod pointing 45° upstream

Angler legering across

Angler legering down the side

Fig. 32. Rod positions when straight legering in flowing water.

The first thing is to use the softest tip that conditions will allow. It may be that the tip you are using is too stiff and the fish are feeling it and dropping the bait before you can connect with them. In conjunction with this, you can try shortening, or on occasions, lengthening the tail. One thing that often works is to increase the size of your hook and bait, using a double maggot instead of a single. Hopefully this will also pick out the bigger fish. Your bite rate may be reduced, but if you do start to hit them at least your catch-rate is improved and this is the important consideration.

**Stuart:**   The other thing you can do is to put on extra weight, say another half ounce or so and wind down to it, so that they hook themselves on the lead. This method is used a lot on the Trent which is full of these small skimmers and where this is a common problem. It also pays to use barbless hooks on these occasions to give you better penetration. Bream can be a pig. They can drive the sanest of men wild. It happens on still water and flowing water. You get these tiny indications and you are saying 'Go on, go on', but they will not have it. They will move in, muck around, you will get line bites, little knocks or even pulling the rod off the rest, but under these conditions it is a waste of time even picking the rod up, because if you foul hook one and loose it, they are gone. But then, all of a sudden they will tip up and get their heads down and decide to have a munch and that's it. My theory with bream fishing is to cast in and sit on my hands. With experience you can pick out the real bites and these are the ones to hit. Often you can get spectators sat behind you, telling you that you have just missed a bite, but you know full well that it was not a proper bite so you leave it alone. At the end of the day these people will tell you that you could have doubled your weight if you had not missed seeing so many bites, but you know that if you had started to try and hit them you would have spooked the shoal and caught even less.

**Maurice:**   Stuart is right about this when fishing for the larger bream and the hookbait is not being touched, but if you are being pestered by these little skimmers and the bait is being continually ragged, under these circumstances you are not going to do any good anyway, even if you catch one occasionally, as they do not weigh very much, so you need to take a positive approach and try to do something about it. What I would do in a situation like that, if I know that they were those little skimmers that don't weigh anything, is to step up the feed rate and try to feed them off and hope to get a better stamp of fish to feed. This is one way out of it. It may not always work, but what have you to lose anyway? because it is no good being sat there getting bite after bite and not getting anything in the net to show for it. Having said that, you must know that your set up is right. Providing you are confident that you are using the right rod and sensitivity of quivertip and that you have rung all of the changes with regards to size and length of tail and hook sizes, then by taking this positive approach you have everything to gain.

With regards to inducing bites, whereas I will twitch the bait on still water, when feeder fishing on flowing water, it is seldom I will move the feeder to induce bites. If I feel that these tactics are necessary on flowing water I will always switch to the straight leger. You can control the way a bomb moves down the swim much better than you can a feeder. Due to the current acting upon the cross sectional area of a feeder, once it is moved, it can take on a life of its own and become totally unpredictable. With a straight lead you have much more control and the important thing is, you can 'feel' it through the swim much better. Often, after taking one or two fish, especially when chub fishing, the fish will drop back down the swim and you need to go down after them. If you were to do this with a feeder there is a chance of the feed and the fish being taken out of your swim into the peg of the man down-stream. This is the last thing you want to happen. In these circumstances, I will always switch to the straight leger, working the bait down the swim in search of where the fish have moved to. If I feel that they are too unsettled to risk disturbing them any more, I will rest the far bank line for a while and switch my attentions to my closer line. I will still feed the far line to try to bring the fish back up and get them feeding confidently again. Whenever I feed on a river, whichever line or lines I decide upon, I will always put my feed into the same place, which will be in front of me on the far line or slightly down-stream on the closer line. If on occasions I ever do cast a feeder further down the swim to establish if the fish have moved down a bit, I will always cast down with an 'empty' feeder. If I establish that the fish have moved down and it is still safe to catch them, I will then switch to the straight leger.

**Stuart:**   Yes I have to agreed, you never want to completely fish out a line, by leaving a few fish still out there they will attract other fish into the swim, and providing you keep the line fed whilst fishing your reserve line, you are going to give them confidence to start feeding again. Fish it out completely and you stand a good chance of killing it for the remainder of the match. This applies of course on both still and flowing water, but more particularly to flowing water, especially on fairly narrow venues where your choice of lines is restricted.

The other way you can induce bites is to keep ringing the changes with your hook baits, trying different hook baits in various combinations. By changing from a bronze maggot to a red maggot, you can often get a few more extra bites. This is very important, especially when bream fishing. Altering your length and size of tail and also your hook size can often put you back in touch with the fish. Many people think that legering is a lazy way of fishing, but like any other type of fishing you only get out of it what you put in. If you just set up, bait up and cast in without touching it again until you get a bite then you will do no good at all. Top match anglers are continually working, constantly ringing the changes to keep in touch with the fish.

**Q** *We have touched briefly there upon feeding tactics. What are your general feeding tactics when fishing flowing waters, and what modifications do you make to your general approach to the reaction or lack of it from the fish? What are the signs to look for?*

**Maurice:** A lot depends upon the time of year and the species you are after. On rivers such as the Warwickshire Avon, the Trent and the Thames, there are far more smaller fish moving about than during the summer months and these will be competing with the larger species for the bait. Under these conditions you would expect to use much more bait than you would during the winter months. You would open by using a fairly large volume feeder and I normally cast about ten feederfulls into the swim, leaving it only long enough for the feeder to empty before bringing it out and repeating the process. Once I have laid this carpet of bait out there I would then take it as it comes. I would expect to catch quite a few smaller fish early on and hope to catch the bigger fish later on in the match. The exception to this is when chub fishing. If I am expecting to catch chub, then these can come on at any time, particularly during the early stages when they will move straight in on the feed. Often, half a dozen or so can be caught immediately, then as a rule the shoal tends to drop back and feed more cautiously. In the case of bream, normally you will have to wait longer for these especially the bigger ones, but the skimmers will tend to feed straight away. Often this is when you will come up against the problem of those un-hittable bites and you just have to soldier on in the hope of the better fish appearing later on.

One thing we have assumed during the course of this discussion is that we are fishing the whole of the match on the leger. This, of course, is seldom the case, especially during the summer months. On many rivers legering and feeder tactics are used in conjunction with conventional float fishing methods and the match will be planned around this. There are of course, certain areas, which due to the nature of the target species and the way they want the bait presented, are out and out feeder or legering venues, but in the main, our feeder fishing and legering is done in conjunction with the float and increasingly more, the pole. The War-wickshire Avon and the Trent are classic examples of this. They are mixed species and mixed method venues. You will be feeding a number of different lines throughout the match, alternating between the lines and the methods used in response to the fish, so as to maintain the catch-rate. Although we will always set up an appropriate leger and feeder rig, there are many occasions when we do not use them. Alternately, there are other occasions when we will also set up float and pole tackle and never use them either. It all comes down to pre-match planning and fish response. You always go into a match with a target weight in mind and use whichever method or combination of methods that will achieve this.

Some anglers do use a more single-minded approach, and consider having too many methods to hand to be a handicap, often confusing the issue. But, again, with our experience we can read the signs and automatically know the right time to change. If we know the match is going to be won with big barbel or bream weights the only float rods we would take with us would be the ones we use for legering.

**Stuart:**   During the winter months we would use legering methods far more, especially when the rivers are carrying extra water, because we know that under these situations they are the best methods of presenting the bait.

Our initial opening tactics would be far more cautious than in summer. We might start off on a larger volume feeder, but only cast it in once between bites. But more usually we would start off with one of the smaller feeders, changing down to a really small one if bites were really slow. If no bites were coming at all we would switch to the straight lead.

Often when chub fishing we will start with a medium feeder but after a couple of casts, switch to a really small one, introducing the barest minimum of feed necessary to keep them interested. Many anglers make the mistake of continuing to use the same feeder althrough the match, not realising that feeding with a feeder is no different to when feeding with a float. You do not keep feeding the same amount of feed althrough a match when float fishing, you measure it to the response of the fish, stepping the amount up and down accordingly. Legering is no different in this respect. If we are fishing within catapult range we always prefer, when the going is hard, to loose feed and use the straight lead. If, due to the range or the accuracy of the feeding, we opt for the feeder, we will always be altering the size of the feeder to suit the response, or lack of it, of the fish. We often cast across with an empty or half-empty feeder if conditions dictate it. We never keep feeding out of habit. Our results tell us we are right.

**Maurice:**   Sometimes we do get it wrong. I remember the last match I fished this season (1989–90). On my way to the peg, an angler whose advice I have always respected, told me to go very easy with the feed.

The current form of the venue pointed to this being the correct approach. As it turned out, I came second in the match, but afterwards I was convinced that had I fished the match my normal way, which would have involved much heavier feeding, I would have won it. On the day I am sure a greater amount of feed would have brought a bigger response but the seeds of doubt had been sown in my mind and I erred on the side of caution. Having said that, I remember many other occasions when my instinct has told me to step up the feed and I have ended up killing the swim.

Unfortunately, with fishing, there are no hard and fast rules and this is what makes it interesting and why we keep on going week in, week out, despite these set-backs and disappointments.

The biggest factor that influences our decisions is the nature of a match. If it is a team event, your tactics will be completely different to when fishing as an individual. There comes a point in most matches when you are struggling and that you have to make a decision whether to carry on as you are, getting the odd fish, or, if you know you are well behind going for broke in the hope of an odd big barbel or bream. In an individual event you do not think twice about this, out goes the meat or the worm and you sit it out. In a team match, your reaction is completely different. You think 'Well, I can't go back to Ken with a dry net'. So up the bank goes the leger rod, out comes the whip, and you scratch around for 2 or 3 lb of bleak. Alright, you may have caught a couple of barbel and won your section, but if you know you can definitely get those bleak then you have to go for them. Such are the vagaries of match fishing.

**Q** *If the anglers around you are catching and you are struggling, what tactics can you employ to try to move the fish from them, into your swim and once you have succeeded, how can you prevent them from doing the same to you?*

**Stuart:**  Praying may help, but a lot depends upon the species you are after. With bream this often happens. It is common, as the bream move around a water, for the anglers around you to start catching whilst you are not. But if you are confident that you have done it right and have got plenty of bait down, then you must be patient and hope that when they do eventually arrive, you will hold them and get more fish out from the shoal before it moves on than the anglers around you have done.

Having said that I always remember talking to Ivan Marks on the Welland, in the 1970's. At that time Maurice and I were fishing for Worcester in the National Championships. Now, although Ivan is still the man now, at that time, he was 'The man' as far as bream venues were concerned, and one of his methods on this water, was to induce the anglers around him to make a mistake. He knew all of the areas and the way that the fish moved around. In those days it was all straight legering, using balls of groundbait and feed. The normal method was to feed half a dozen balls in at the start and then sit it out until the fish arrived. When they did, it was usual for two or three anglers to be catching in a line. Now because of his reputation, even though they were catching, all eyes would be on Ivan to see what he was doing. Now, if these lads who were catching were four or five pegs away, Ivan would start balling groundbait in. The anglers who were catching would think 'Ah, ah, if I don't put in some more feed, Ivan is going to have all of these fish'. So, of course, they would start putting groundbait in on top of this shoal of bream, which, as we know now, would unsettle them. Once this happened, Ivan would, of course, stop feeding and as the fish moved down, swingtips would be flying up along the stretch, due to line bites caused by the fish moving through, and as the anglers were striking into these false bites, the fish would be spooked again until eventually they would arrive at Ivan's peg. He would be sitting there with his arms folded, chuckling at what had happened, and knowing full well that providing he did not disturb the fish anymore they would settle down and he had got enough feed down to hold them for the duration of the match. Anglers either side would still be balling in groundbait to try to hold these fish, but by then it would be too late, and the disturbance they were causing only made the fish more determined to stay where they were, in front of Ivan. Of course, whenever these tactics succeeded, the outcome of the match was just a formality. As I have said, he was inducing them to make a mistake, and when you think about it, he was dead right.

Nowadays, top anglers are far more educated and it is less likely that you would succeed in making them do the same, but if you feel that you need more feed out there, then the time to do it is before the fish get too close to you, and if it encourages the other anglers who are catching to make a mistake, then all well and good.

**Maurice:** Yes, fish, especially bream and carp, will move around on a water as will roach on occasions, but on a river it is far more difficult. You can bring roach and bream up-stream from the next peg providing the river is fairly uniform in depth, but with chub it is much harder, they will move, but they won't move far. If you have chub in your swim, it is because they live there and unless the cover they are using such as over-hanging branches or rushes etc., extends all the way along the far bank they are not going to move. By firing bait down the swim, you will sometimes encourage fish up from the swim down-stream, and I remember a particular example when I won the Wye Championships. I drew a peg at Field Farm, two pegs above a ford and 'The peg' was the peg below me, and one of the best Wye anglers, Austin Clissett, was on it. He was feeding small balls of groundbait with a catapult, and was catching odd chub. For two hours I never had a fish and Austin was catching steadily. I then did the only thing I could do. I balled it in, because I knew it was the only way I was going to draw any fish off of him. There were obviously no fish present in my swim at that time, so what had I to lose. Having said that I was confident that it was a day when it could happen. Sure enough they moved up and in the last two hours I had about thirty chub for 52 lb. Now, if Austin had put in the same amount of feed as I had done, I would not have won it. The reason he didn't was that he did not want to risk driving them up onto my feed. Unfortunately for him on the day, these fish wanted plenty of feed and once he realised that they had moved up to me it was too late to do anything about it. Whilst it is possible to move fish up-stream on flowing water, you cannot move them down-stream. This is just one instance when my tactics paid off. You could do the same thing time and time again and it would not happen and you would kill it stone dead. The advantage I had on this occasion was that the two swims were of even depth and the fish were prepared to move.

**Stuart:** This eveness is the important thing. If say you, Maurice and myself were fishing in a line on the Warwickshire Avon, and I was on the down-stream peg and it had a feature opposite such as a bush overhanging a bay. Now if you are a chub, you will want to live under the bush in the bay, and there is no way you are going to move. So, no matter what Maurice or yourself did, you would not be able to move my fish out of the peg. The same thing will happen if the river bed alters in depth.

I fished a match at Kensey once, and 'The peg' was just around the corner, peg 26, and I drew up-stream on peg 25. I spoke to one of the local cracks and he said to me 'You are 15 yards off winning the match'. I asked him if he thought they would move up and he doubted it very much. On this stretch, you only fish a third of the way out, so I cast a feeder well down-stream at the end of my peg. The only problem was, the peg gradually shallowed up, it was a kind of spoon shaped and where I was, it was 12 or 13 ft deep and rising, but in the next peg it was only 7 ft and of course that was where the fish were. Despite all of my efforts to move them I failed. I only had one fish, and that just happened to be the only one that lived there!

On a broad, seemingly featureless river such as the Trent, then providing the depth is even you can sometimes move the fish up-stream from the peg below, but even then there are occasions where some sort of hidden feature below the surface is what attracts the fish to live there, and no matter what you do they just will not move. In these situations you have to re-sign yourself to being pegged next to the winner.

**Q**   *How do you fish the deep fast flowing rivers such as the Wye, the lower Severn and the tidal Trent. How do you cope with flood conditions when all sorts of debris are coming down-stream with the current?*

**Maurice:**   These are the conditions when you need to fish the large capacity feeders with up to 4 oz of lead on them in conjunction with the more powerful rods. Due to the pace of the current the feed soon gets washed away down-stream and these rivers will stand a lot of feed. On the tidal rivers you often need to have several rods of different ranges of sensitivity set up, especially when you expect the tide to change during the course of the match. You do need to know when the tide is going to change so you can plan your match accordingly. This often means that during the course of the match, the river will change direction with regards to the flow, and at some period during the match, it is going to be stood. Your feeding tactics will obviously alter as the conditions alter and you must be very careful in your response to these or you will lose your fish to the anglers pegged either side of you. On a day when the fish are feeding well, as the rate of flow alters and begins to slow down, then this is the time to step up the feed rate, concentrating it in front of you and gradually altering its position slightly down-stream in anticipation of the tide turning, when of course this position will become the upstream position. During the short period when the river is stood, this is the time, if ground baiting tactics are being used, to introduce your balls of groundbait and feed, but you will still use a heavy stiff mix to prevent it from being washed away once the flow picks up again after the change. During this period I would switch to a light straight leger or even waggler tactics until the river starts to move again.

Many anglers who do not do their homework, often get caught out during these changes. They will not have their groundbait mixed ready and then lose a lot of time having to mix it. By the time they have got it ready, the river is already starting to pull off again and they have missed the opportunity to get the feed in and down to exactly the right place.

When fishing these heavy flows you will always fish the drop-back method generally associated with flowing water. Your hook lengths will be stepped up to match the power of your rods and if you still need to use small hooks with small baits these will be of the forged variety to match the strength of the hook lengths and to hold the fish in these heavy flows.

**Stuart:**   The same sorts of tactics need to be used in flood conditions, but here you have an additional problem. Debris of all kinds will be coming down with the the current, getting caught up on the line. Under these conditions you need to use far more lead than is normal to hold bottom, otherwise as soon as you get a bit of weed on the line the increased pressure will move the feeder and you will be plagued with false bites. The other problem you have is the rubbish running down the line clogging up your link and bait. If your bait keeps getting covered with rubbish there is no way you will get a bite. This can be overcome quite easily, by putting a leger stop on the line above the link. This will act as a focal point around which the debris catching onto your line will stop and collect. This will help to prevent the rubbish going right down to your hook length and covering the bait.

You will not be able to hold the tackle out as long as you may like to, but by using more lead you can at least hold it out that bit longer before the weight of the rubbish moves the feeder. Because it is being concentrated around the leger stop it is easier to clear and helps you to get back into the water more quickly. I often find that the knot formed by tying my double loop rig is often sufficient to stop the rubbish going down to my terminal tackle and I do not need to use a leger stop. Again trail and error will teach you what you need to do.

**Maurice:** In these sort of conditions you are normally fishing down the side with maggot or out in the flow with luncheon meat or lobworm. When using the meat or lobworm you will normally be using heavy leads out in the flow, though on occasions it can pay you if the fish are still feeding well to use a large block-end in conjunction with the heavy ski leads. You will still use a big bait on the hook if the river holds a decent head of larger fish such as barbel or chub.

Many anglers fish too negatively when faced with flood conditions. They often fail to realise that these bigger fish will still be out in mid-river and often still feed under these conditions. Providing you step up your weight as Stuart has explained and you are using a rod capable of handling this heavy tackle, this method does work well. You must fish positively. Many anglers when faced with several feet of flood water tend to give up before they start, resigning themselves to failure. By taking this more positive approach then providing you have fish in front of you, you can catch two or three of these bigger fish and win the match.

Despite the fact that you will be picking up a lot of debris on the line, the bites when they do come are normally vicious bites and all you have to do is pick up the rod and the fish is on. There is nothing you can do to stop rubbish collecting on the line, although by using a stop as Stuart has mentioned, you can at least keep most of it off of your terminal tackles so that your bait is clear. You have no alternative but to keep reeling in and clearing it off the line when it gets too much. If the conditions are so bad that it is impossible to fish out in the flow, the only thing you can do then is to try to find a bit of a slack area in front of you and fish a maggot or a worm on the straight lead down the side, under your feet. This happened to me this year on the River Trent at Newton-Solney and I drew a peg on the inside of a bend and this sort of thing was happening on that day. The river was two or three feet up and everything was ripping down with the current. It was impossible to hold out, even for a minute, there was that much rubbish coming down. In the end I fished a big feeder right under my feet behind my keep-net and I just couldn't believe it. I finished up with 12 pounds of chub.

**Stuart:** Sometimes on these occasions it can be worse fishing on the inside than out in the river. You can draw these sort of pegs such as on the mud-flats at Beauchamp Court and you would think with the river pulling away from you, you would have a nice clear slack inside, but you then get these dead leaves rolling around in front of you and it's virtually impossible to fish it under these conditions.

I remember the match when I was second this year on the Wye Championships, with 30 eels for 10 lb. When we started fishing there was about 6 ft of extra water in and by the end of the match there was over 12 ft. We were sat right at the top of the bank watching it come up. I used this really big lead and wound down to it and whenever it moved I wound in. Sometimes there was a fish on the end and sometimes there wasn't, it was that sort of day.

With living in this area we have had a lot of experience of fishing flooded rivers. It is amazing how they vary in form from one to the other. On the Warwickshire Avon, very few areas respond well under flood conditions but on the Severn a number of anglers love it when it comes up a bit. They fish up to 5 or 6 oz leads to hold the bait out in the flow using the luncheon meat, and they are very successful. As Maurice has said, don't be deceived into thinking that the fish always come into the edge during flood conditions. Barbel especially are designed to live out in these conditions and need the minimum of effort to hold out in the stronger water.

We are used to really heavy gear such as a 6 lb line straight through and big leads. Look in the tackle box of anglers, particularly Northern anglers, and I doubt if they possess anything bigger than 1 oz, but anglers around here carry pieces of lead gas pipes around to cope with the conditions we often need to face. I know many anglers who fish the Thames and they always prefer to fish for bream when the river is well up and the colour of chocolate. I remember a few years ago when a group came up to fish the Clive Smith Memorial Match, here on the Severn and the river was well up with trees coming down and all sorts. They were really looking forward to fishing it under these conditions, until we told them that unlike Thames bream, Severn bream did not feed under these conditions. But at least they had the tackle to cope with the conditions.

We often see teams from other areas coming to practice when there is a National Championships on the Severn, and unless they have been on the river before, most of them do not have the tackle to cope when the river is carrying extra water.

# Match Experiences

**Q** *Finally, to put some of the points we have covered into perspective, I would like you to think back and tell me about any particular match, successful or otherwise, where you had to work particularly hard and make a lot of changes and adjustments to find and keep in touch with the fish, explaining what you had to do and why you did it? Also where appropriate, what mistakes you made and with hindsight how you could have perhaps improved upon your final result?*

**Maurice:** I can tell you about a couple of matches, one where I fed very little in comparison to the other anglers and another where I fed far more heavily. The first was the qualifying round of the Daily Mirror lead-free 'Save the Swans' competition fished on the lower-Severn at Oak Meadows. In this particular match you had to get into the top four to qualify for the final which was to be held at Longleat lakes. There were about 120 anglers competing in the match and with the peg I drew I didn't think I stood a very good chance of qualifying. It was an area where I thought I could catch one or two fish but not good enough to get me there.

The first thing I did when I got to the peg was to see who had drawn around me, and fortunately for me there was a very good local angler who drew above me and I knew that this particular chap was going to feed a lot of bait. I knew what he was going to feed because I went up to his peg to have a look and he was going to feed caster and hemp. Now, on this day the river was carrying an extra foot of water and was flowing fairly hard. So what I decided to do was to fish a tiny little feeder with a lot of weight on it. The feeder itself would only take about a dozen or so maggots and I intended a half pint of feed to last the whole match. My intention was to fish on his feed, so I picked the same line as he fished casting slightly up-stream with plenty of weight on to hold and by allowing a bow to form I was fishing for drop-backs. In conjunction with this I fished a 5 ft hook length with a 22 barbless hook and a single maggot and I only used a handful of maggots all day. I just had an odd fish now and again as they dropped back off of his feed. Now he was pulling his hair out because he could not catch and I was catching, but it wasn't until it was too late that he realised what was happening.

Now that was one day when I actually got it right and it worked. I ended up with 19 lb for third place which put me into the final and if I remember right, in the final itself luckily I came third again and won £1,500. But it was one day where it was the type of venue and the type of conditions which dictated the use of a lot of feed and I opted for the exact opposite approach and it paid off, and it was also one of those rare occasions where I fished to a plan and it worked.

The other match I remember was where I did the exact opposite. This was on the River Weaver and it was a very important match. It was the 1985 Semi-finals of the *Angling Times* Winter League and this of course was a team match. We had all been down the week before practising and we found that it was a very wide, deep river and it held a good head of quality roach. Now this river is sluice controlled and we found that when they ran it off, the top couple of feet would start to move, but the main part of the river would remain almost motionless. If you float fished it with the waggler it would give you the impression that it was flowing quite hard, but your feed would go a couple of feet down-stream and then fall almost straight down to the bottom. This meant that if you were loose-feeding for the float, you would not be getting any feed to where you were actually fishing. The other teams were also reluctant to feed very heavily, so virtually no feed at all was actually going down the peg. On this basis we knew that the lead was going to be a better bet than the waggler with regards to bait presentation, knowing that we would be fishing over our feed. So we fed far heavier than any other team that were competing, fishing the straight lead over our loose feed. The chap next to me put about half a pint of bait in over the course of the match and I put in about three pints and in the last two hours these roach moved in on my feed. We were of course fishing underneath where we fed whilst the opposition were fishing well down from their feed, thinking that this was where it was going. One thing that helped was that the fish did not feed until the latter stages of the match when it was too late for the opposition to suss out what was happening. Half way through the match, I only had two gudgeon in the net and the lad from Izaak Walton pegged next to me had about eight gudgeon, and he really thought he was hammering me. In the last two hours I then put 7 lb of roach in the net and as a team we totally annihilated the opposition, not only winning the team event, but also taking the first four individual places. This demonstrates the importance of pre-match planning and practice.

Fig. 33. Maurice with his 7 lb 1 oz catch of River Weaver roach that gave him 2nd individual place in the Superteam's historic victory in the 1985 *Angling Times* Winter League semi-final, using leger tactics with the Sigma Wand.

**Stuart:**   The match that comes to mind whilst being one of my biggest successes, was in retrospect also one of my biggest failures. Had I fished the peg positively in the beginning and changed my tactics towards the end of the match I feel certain, and honestly believe that I could have caught over 100 lb in an English match which would have been a major achievement. It was the day of the Wye Championships in 1983. We had just got back from winning the Captain Morgan final in Ireland on the Thursday. As you can imagine, I was still full of rum and Cokes and I had still not got my feet back to ground level. The match was on the Sunday and I drew this peg at Carrots in a big dead bay and they call it 'Dead man's hole'. I had drawn this peg before on a previous Wye Championship when Maurice had won it with 56lbs. On that occasion I started the match fishing bread and lucheon meat on a big balsa float down the middle of the river and hooked a couple of chub and lost both of them. This killed the swim, and I ended up fishing the maggot for dace and I finished with a very poor weight.

Obviously, I was not very happy at drawing this peg again, and the only reason I stuck at it was because my dad had drawn the peg up-stream and as big as I was he would have kicked my back-side if I didn't try my best! So I started fishing on the inside of this big dead bay which runs opposite to the main flow. I caught nothing in the first one and a half hours but I had also been feeding 30 yards out in the middle of the main river, which was about 11ft deep and going like an express train. I changed to a big 9 swan bread float down the middle and I started to catch chub at a very good rate. At 2.30 p.m. with half an hour of the match still to go something went wrong and I stopped catching. I think the wind may have changed direction a bit and I couldn't put the float through to them properly and get the bait to the right place and I am sure to this day that if I had changed to the straight lead with luncheon meat or to the feeder with the caster and plonked it in amongst them I would have had 100–120 lb. I finished up with 85 lb– 15oz, one pound clear of the next man who had 84 lb–15 oz. I beat him by an exact one pound, but it could have gone either way. The annoying thing was that I had a feeder rod made up ready on the bank behind me but did not think to use it, and this has eaten away at me ever since.

Another match I remember very well is one that I wouldn't have done much good in had not Maurice drawn the next peg to me. This was at Newton-Solney on the Upper-Trent. I drew peg 21. I said 'This is alright Maurice, what have you drawn?'. He said '22'. 'Sorry mate', I said 'but that's crap really'. Anyway, I knew I had to fish for barbel on the feeder but when I checked in my box, I found that I'd left my box of feeders back home in Worcester. So I borrowed a few feeders off Maurice and a few off of the other lads and off we went to the pegs. I started fishing on the feeder, feeding hemp and casters with casters on the hook. I was using a 6 lb mainline and a 3lb hooklength with a single caster on a size 20 forged hook. I had a bad snag in my swim and I had to plonk it up-stream and let it come behind the snag and if you got it right you would get the odd bite. After the first hour I had three barbel for about 9 lb. Anyway Maurice came up from his 'duff' peg after about one and a half hours to see what I'd caught and so I told him and as I was talking, I lifted up the rod to wind in and this fish suddenly hit the bait, nearly pulling the rod out of my hand. It felt a really big fish, about 5 or 6 lb and I felt it dive into this weed bed and it just parted company. Bearing in mind I was fishing 6 lb to a 3 lb hook length, well normally you can get an elephant in on that. Maurice said 'Hang on there we'll soon stop that', and he came back with his President rod with 6 lb line straight through to a size 12 hook. He must have struggled to tie the line on to this 12 hook with the thickness of this line, the coils on the knot seemed massive. I said,

'Maurice, no fish in its right mind is going to grab that'.

'Put it in' he insisted.

'No way' I said 'I can't do that', and I replaced my size 20 hook and the 3lb hook length and cast it back in. In the meantime Maurice had gone back to his peg, leaving the rod on the bank behind me. Anyway I had a couple more fish without losing any when Maurice came back up.

'How are you doing?' he asked.

I told him I'd had a couple more and had about 15 lb in the net.

'You haven't used that rod yet then'.

I said 'No' and as I said it, I wound in only to find I had blunted the point of the hook. No way could I get a caster to go on it without bursting it. So I thought 'Right, whilst I'm putting another caster on I will sling this rig of Maurice's out and keep him happy'. I put three casters on this size 12 hook to try and disguise it a bit and cast it in. I worked it around to the end of the snag and before I could put the rod on the rest, the tip banged over and all hell broke loose. I just couldn't believe it. I hadn't had a bite on a 3 lb line and a size 20 for about an hour and here I was straight into them on 6lb line and a size 12 hook! I had another four fish on this heavy rig and of course I could do what I liked with them, pull them through weed beds, anything, no way could they break me on this 6 lb line. I finished the match with 39 lb–15 oz which gave me second place. My lost barbel didn't cost me the match, as it was won with an incredible 85 lbs of chub.

This just goes to show that on occasions a more positive approach with bigger baits and heavier tackle can be the method when the fish are feeding well, and can give you an advantage in a snaggy swim when bigger fish are around. What is the point of hooking fish you cannot get out. Better to hook fewer, but put more weight in the net, although on this day my catch rate actually increased.

# BEWARE

# OVERHEAD ELECTRIC POWER LINES

## WARNING!

Living for fishing is one thing. Dying for it, or maiming yourself for life, is quite another. The one blot on the history and development of pole fishing in the last decade has been the number of serious accidents involving poles and overhead power lines.

The new carbon poles are frighteningly efficient at conducting electricity. They are long enough nowadays to make contact with power lines, but they do not even need to connect. Get one near enough and the power arcs across, with devastating results.

Fellow anglers have been killed. Two friends of ours have been horribly burned, and one has lost part of a leg. It should never have happened; it cannot happen to you or to us? But of course it can, unless you and we take the greatest of care.

So obey warning notices, and the advice from the electricity generating industry and the National Federation of Anglers to LOOK OUT and LOOK UP whenever you even think about setting up pole tackle in an area you are not familiar with.

Perhaps the reason why "lightning" never strikes twice is that it does not usually have to....

**PLEASE DON'T DIE FOR YOUR FISHING!**